30-minute Vegetarian

30-minute Vegetarian

Joanna Farrow

Photography by William Reavell

Bounty Books

First published in Great Britain in 1998 by Hamlyn,
a division of Octopus Publishing Group Ltd.
This Revised edition first published 2004

This edition published 2005 by Bounty Books,
a division of Octopus Publishing Group Ltd
2–4 Heron Quays, London E14 4JP

ISBN 0 7537 1262 8
ISBN 13 9780753712627

A CIP catalogue record for this book is available
from the British Library

Printed and bound in China

NOTES

1 The Department of Health advises that eggs should not be consumed raw. It is prudent for more vulnerable people such as pregnant and nursing mothers, invalids, the elderly, babies and young children to avoid uncooked or lightly cooked dishes made with eggs.

2 Meat and poultry should be cooked thoroughly. To test if poultry is cooked, pierce the flesh through the thickest part with a skewer or fork – the juices should run clear, never pink or red.

3 This book includes dishes made with nuts and nut derivatives. It is advisable for those with known allergic reactions to nuts and nut derivatives and those who may be potentially vulnerable to these allergies, such as pregnant and nursing mothers, invalids, the elderly, babies and children, to avoid dishes made with nuts and nut oils. It is also prudent to check the labels of pre-prepared ingredients for the possible inclusion of nut derivatives.

contents

introduction

30 Minute Vegetarian will appeal to anyone who knows how exotic and exciting contemporary vegetarian cooking can be.

Like many children of my generation, I was raised on a meat-based diet, but even then I found a traditional roast dinner or a classic winter stew rather difficult to swallow, despite my mother's evident cooking skills. I have memories of trying to hide unwanted pieces of beef or lamb under my knife and fork in the naive hope that my parents would not notice. This was possibly a taste of things to come for me personally, but maybe the reality is that most of us have moved away from the once-standard 'meat and two veg' diet.

This is, of course, an inevitable consequence of the explosion of interest in all things relating to food. We travel more and seize the opportunity to sample different cuisines, new flavours and ingredients that were completely alien to our parents. There is also now a far greater variety of foods widely available, gathered from all over the world. Television programmes, food magazines and cookery books all fuel our desire to enjoy an ever-widening feast of interesting flavours.

All this has helped the vegetarian cause tremendously. Moral issues aside, people have discovered that there are many non-meat based cuisines around the globe from which to draw new inspiration, and so meat (like my mother's roasts) has been pushed to one side. How many people eat as much meat as they did even ten years ago?

My aim in this book is to show that vegetarian cooking has thrown off its dull yet worthy image, epitomized by the token vegetable lasagne or the equally dreary vegetarian alternatives that some restaurants used to (and still do in some cases) offer. Whether you are a confirmed vegetarian or seeking a fresh approach, here is a collection of recipes to excite and delight – a heady mix of stimulating flavours and diverse culinary practices. And it is all fast food! It takes very little time to whizz up a delicious homemade pesto and toss it with pasta, or to throw a blend of aromatic Far Eastern spices in a pan with beans and vegetables, then pile them on to noodles. This spontaneity captures the essence of fresh herbs and the pungency of spices to create imaginative, flavourful dishes in less than 30 minutes. Yes, you might have to plan what you are going to cook a little more, and yes, it might mean using a few more ingredients, but it certainly will not involve you in spending hours in the kitchen assembling complicated or expensive creations.

For anyone who is yet to be convinced about the value of vegetarian cooking, think of your meat-based diet as a habit. Once you break the habit of meat-eating, it is not necessarily a case of giving up anything but opening yourself up to a wealth of new, vibrant and easy ways of cooking.

Joanna
Farrow

glossary

Balsamic vinegar This has been a popular ingredient for some years now, with a far richer, sweeter flavour than ordinary wine vinegars (although these still have their uses in many dishes). It is made in Modena, Italy and is aged in wooden barrels for anything up to 50 years, the maturing time developing its flavour and price!

Cheeses Cheese plays an important role in vegetarian cooking, not purely as a flavouring but as a useful source of protein, calcium and vitamins. While many vegetarians will eat non-vegetarian cheeses, others avoid it because of the presence of rennet used to solidify many cheeses. In recent years, there has been a huge increase in the number of cheeses produced using vegetarian rennet. The difference in taste is barely discernible and it behaves no differently when used in cooking.

Brie and Camembert: These are encased in a soft, white penicillin mould and vary considerably from dry and crumbly to runny and strongly flavoured. Sliced, they can be lightly grilled and tossed with pasta or used as a topping for toast, pizzas or pastries.

Haloumi: This firm, salty Greek cheese has a dense, chewy texture that is delicious grilled or fried and tossed into salads. It goes particularly well with fruit, such as grapes and pears.

Mascarpone: A deliciously soft, velvet-smooth cream cheese made with cows' milk. It is good in savoury dishes since it melts to create wonderfully rich sauces, as well as in sweet dishes as a creamy trifle or tiramisu base.

Mozzarella: A fresh, moist, subtle-flavoured cheese, made from either buffalo or cows' milk. It has an inviting stringy quality when melted and is often combined with more intensely flavoured cheeses, such as Parmesan, to add flavour. Excellent on pizzas or pastries, or in salads.

Parmesan: A strongly flavoured hard, salty cheese which is matured for years to develop the full flavour. Always buy in a block rather than ready-grated. Leftovers can be grated and frozen.

Ricotta: A soft, bland, fresh cheese that is often stirred into pasta or used in pastry fillings. It is also delicious as a sweet and makes a very quick and easy dessert. Try mixing it with chocolate, ginger, dried fruit and liqueurs.

Chillies These vary considerably in heat intensity and unfortunately there is often no way of knowing how hot they are until you cook them. As a rough guide, the tiny Thai chillies, both red and green, are always very fiery, while the larger, chubbier chillies, usually sold loose in supermarkets, tend to be milder. Sometimes more unusual chillies, such as Scotch Bonnet and Habañero, are available in small packs, usually labelled as to heat intensity.

Coconut Once you have mastered the art of opening a fresh coconut, the grated flesh adds a refreshing, nutty flavour to salads and stir-fries. To open the coconut, first pierce the three 'eyes' with a skewer (sometimes a corkscrew works well) and drain the juice into a mug. Some people love this nutritious, opaque juice, while others hate it! Place the coconut in a plastic carrier bag and beat with a hammer to crack it into several pieces. Ease out the flesh from the shell.

Coconut milk This is not the juice from inside the whole coconut, but a thick, velvety smooth, creamy milk that is processed from coconut flesh. Sold in cans and cartons, it is one of the most widely used cooking liquids in South-east Asian and Caribbean cookery, and excellent for giving 'body' and richness to vegetarian soups, stews and oriental dishes.

Creamed coconut Very concentrated in flavour, a small chunk (about 25–50 g/1–2 oz) can be added to soups, stews and sauces to thicken and intensify flavour. Creamed coconut melts as it heats up.

Lemon grass This is now widely available fresh and adds a wonderful, aromatic, lemony flavour to soups and spicy dishes. Peel away any tough, discoloured leaves, then finely slice or chop the rest. If you cannot find fresh lemon grass, look for it dried in jars with the other spices.

Noodles There are many different types of noodle available, from rice noodles to those made from wheat, bean starch and buckwheat. Some are thick and ribbon-like, while others are fine like vermicelli. They generally cook very quickly and rice noodles will turn mushy and paste-like if overcooked.

Olive oil Extra virgin olive oil comes from the first cold pressing of the olives, giving a rich flavour and deep colour. Subsequent pressings produce oils of a lighter flavour. It is worth keeping an extra virgin olive oil for salad dressings and dishes in which you want an intense, Mediterranean flavour, and a lighter, cheaper one for other cooking and for frying.

You can easily make your own flavoured oils by steeping sprigs of rosemary, tarragon, thyme, bay leaves or some whole fresh chillies in the oil for a few weeks before using.

Pasta This is a blend of flour and water, sometimes with the addition of egg. Fresh pasta has a better flavour and texture than dried and cooks very quickly, usually in less time than packet directions suggest, so take care when cooking. Leftover fresh pasta can be frozen successfully. Dried pasta makes a good storecupboard alternative but brands vary considerably in quality. When draining any cooked pasta, always leave the last of the cooking water clinging to the pasta, to prevent the dish from being dry.

Pesto This is a blend of basil, pine nuts, Parmesan cheese, garlic and oil which can be bought in jars or, preferably, homemade. Simply put a clove of chopped garlic, a handful of basil leaves, 3 tablespoons pine nuts and 50 g/2 oz grated Parmesan cheese in a food processor or blender and process, gradually adding a little olive oil, to make a thick, oily paste. Pesto is delicious simply tossed with pasta for a quick and easy supper, or stirred into soups and sauces. Red pesto has tomatoes added to the basic recipe.

Sun-dried tomato pesto (see page 65) makes a delicious variation on the pesto theme.

Polenta This is made from ground maize kernels and is cooked blended with water to make a thick paste. Serve it soft, rather like mashed potatoes, or spread on a tray, leave to set, then slice for grilling or baking, preferably with a cheese topping. Its bland flavour can be enhanced by the addition of garlic, olive oil, herbs, saffron or chillies. Buy packs labelled 'instant polenta' which cooks much faster.

Rice There are dozens of varieties available. Most cook quickly, making a useful alternative to pasta and potatoes, although some varieties of red, brown and 'wild' rice take much longer. For spicy dishes, choose white or brown basmati rice or Thai fragrant rice, which has a softer, fluffier texture and better flavour than ordinary long-grain rice. Italian risotto rices, either arborio or carnaroli, are very popular for making classic, creamy risottos. Flavour with mushrooms, asparagus or simply cheese for a quick and easy vegetarian meal.

Rocket

This is a delicious peppery-tasting salad leaf. Try growing your own rather than buying ridiculously expensive small supermarket packs. Sow some in a pot or in the garden monthly throughout the summer for a cheap and far more flavourful supply.

Saffron

It is very expensive, but saffron adds a distinctive flavour and colour to many dishes that no other spice can imitate. It is perfect for Mediterranean rice and bean dishes, or for adding to polenta and potatoes.

Sun-dried tomatoes

These intensely flavoured dried tomatoes, usually bought in oil, are so useful in northern climates where ordinary tomatoes generally lack the colour and sweet flavour of those grown around the Mediterranean. Chopped up, they are great for adding flavour intensity to tomato soups and vegetable stews. Sun-dried tomato paste is equally useful.

Tapenade

A paste-like blend of olives, garlic, capers and olive oil that can be shop-bought or made at home by simply blending 3 tablespoons capers, 75 g/3 oz pitted black olives, 6 tablespoons olive oil and a little garlic, herbs and seasoning. If buying, check that the brand does not contain anchovies.

Tofu

Made from soya beans and sold in block form, tofu is bland in both taste and appearance, but should not be disregarded. Its assets are its nutritional value as a meat replacement and its great versatility in vegetarian cooking. Use it as a carrier for strongly flavoured ingredients such as soy sauce, garlic, ginger, lemon grass and spices. It is also available smoked.

Silken tofu is a lighter version of regular tofu. Easy to mash or blend, it is generally used in drinks and as a dairy replacement in desserts.

Vegetable stock

A vital ingredient in vegetarian soups, stews, casseroles, rice and vegetable dishes. Liquid stock concentrate, bought in small jars, has a better flavour than the reconstituted cubes for everyday vegetarian cooking. For special occasions, buy fresh vegetable stock or make your own if you have time. Use the vegetables listed below as a guide, but throw in any other leftover vegetable trimmings, such as cabbage, broccoli, courgettes, fennel, spring onions or celeriac. Both the colour and flavour of homemade vegetable stock is rich and intense.

Makes 1 litre/1¾ pints

2 tablespoons olive oil
1 large onion, chopped, plus skins
2 carrots, chopped
125 g/4 oz turnip or parsnip
3 celery sticks, sliced
125 g/4 oz mushrooms, sliced
2 bay leaves
several thyme and parsley sprigs
2 tomatoes, chopped
2 teaspoons black peppercorns

one Heat the oil in a large saucepan. Add the onion, carrots, turnip or parsnip, celery and mushrooms and fry gently for 5 minutes. Add the herbs, tomatoes, peppercorns and onion skins and cover with 1.8 litres/3 pints water. **two** Bring to the boil, partially cover and simmer gently for 1 hour. Cool, then strain and refrigerate for up to 2 days.

soups

Soups are without doubt among the easiest, most comforting ways to enjoy vegetarian food. Generous portions thick with chunky vegetables or pulses and served with warm, grainy bread make really satisfying main-meal dishes, while smoothly blended, light and fragrant versions whet the appetite for a delicious meal to follow.

green lentil soup with spiced butter

preparation time **7 mins**
cooking time **23 mins**
total time **30 mins** serves **4**

3 tablespoons olive oil
2 onions, sliced
2 bay leaves
175 g/6 oz green lentils, rinsed
1 litre/1¾ pints Vegetable Stock
   (see page 9)
½ teaspoon ground turmeric
small handful of coriander,
   roughly chopped
salt and pepper

SPICED BUTTER
50 g/2 oz lightly salted butter, softened
1 large garlic clove, crushed
1 teaspoon paprika
1 teaspoon cumin seeds
1 red chilli, deseeded and thinly sliced

one Heat the oil in a saucepan. Add the onions and fry for 3 minutes. Add the bay leaves, lentils, stock and turmeric. Bring to the boil, then reduce the heat, cover and simmer for 20 minutes until the lentils are tender and turning mushy.
two Meanwhile, to prepare the spiced butter, beat the butter with the garlic, paprika, cumin seeds and chilli and transfer to a small serving dish.
three Stir the coriander into the soup, season to taste with salt and pepper and serve with the spiced butter at the table for stirring into the soup.

butter bean and sun-dried tomato soup

preparation time **5 mins**
cooking time **20 mins**
total time **25 mins** serves **4**

3 tablespoons olive oil
1 onion, finely chopped
2 celery sticks, thinly sliced
2 garlic cloves, thinly sliced
2 x 425 g/14 oz cans butter beans, rinsed and
   drained
4 tablespoons sun-dried tomato paste
900 ml/1½ pints Vegetable Stock
   (see page 9)
1 tablespoon chopped rosemary or thyme
salt and pepper
Parmesan cheese shavings, to serve

one Heat the oil in a saucepan. Add the onion and fry for 3 minutes until softened. Add the celery and garlic and fry for 2 minutes.
two Add the butter beans, sun-dried tomato paste, stock, rosemary or thyme and a little salt and pepper. Bring to the boil, then reduce the heat, cover and simmer gently for 15 minutes. Serve sprinkled with the Parmesan shavings.

Although it takes only a few minutes to prepare, this chunky soup distinctly resembles a robust Italian minestrone. It makes a worthy main course served with bread and plenty of Parmesan cheese.

new potato, coriander and leek soup

preparation time **5 mins**
cooking time **20 mins**
total time **25 mins** serves **4**

500 g/1 lb waxy new potatoes, such as Jersey
  Royals, scrubbed
3 small leeks, trimmed
40 g/1½ oz butter
1 tablespoon black mustard seeds
1 onion, chopped
1 garlic clove, thinly sliced
1 litre/1¾ pints Vegetable Stock
  (see page 9)
plenty of freshly grated nutmeg
small handful of coriander, roughly chopped
salt and pepper
warm bread, to serve

one Halve each potato, or cut into 1 cm/½ inch
slices if large. Halve the leeks lengthways,
then cut them across into thin shreds.
two Melt the butter in a heavy-based
saucepan. Add the mustard seeds, onion,
garlic and potatoes and fry gently for
5 minutes. Add the stock and nutmeg and
bring just to the boil. Reduce the heat, cover
and simmer gently for about 10 minutes until
the potatoes are just tender.
three Stir in the leeks and coriander and
cook for a further 5 minutes. Season to
taste with salt and pepper and serve with
warm bread.

black bean soup with soba noodles

preparation time **5 mins**
cooking time **10 mins**
total time **15 mins** serves **4**

200 g/7 oz dried soba noodles
2 tablespoons groundnut or vegetable oil
1 bunch of spring onions, sliced
2 garlic cloves, roughly chopped
1 red chilli, deseeded and sliced
4 cm/1½ inch piece of fresh root ginger,
  peeled and grated
125 ml/4 fl oz black bean sauce or
  black bean stir-fry sauce
750 ml/1¼ pints Vegetable Stock (see page 9)
200 g/7 oz pak choi or spring greens, shredded
2 teaspoons soy sauce
1 teaspoon caster sugar
50 g/2 oz raw, unsalted shelled peanuts

one Cook the noodles in plenty of boiling
water for about 5 minutes until just tender.
two Meanwhile, heat the oil in a saucepan.
Add the spring onions and garlic and fry
gently for 1 minute.
three Add the chilli, ginger, black bean
sauce and stock and bring to the boil. Stir
in the pak choi or spring greens, soy sauce,
sugar and peanuts, reduce the heat and
simmer gently, uncovered, for 4 minutes.
four Drain the noodles and pile into four
serving bowls. Ladle the soup over the
noodles and serve immediately.

Soba noodles, traditional in Japanese cooking, are made
of buckwheat and wholemeal flour, giving them a nutty
flavour without the dryness of many wholemeal pastas.

spinach and mushroom soup

preparation time **5 mins**
cooking time **20 mins**
total time **25 mins** serves **4**

50 g/2 oz butter
1 tablespoon groundnut or vegetable oil
1 onion, finely chopped
150 g/5 oz shiitake mushrooms
175 g/6 oz chestnut or cup mushrooms
2 garlic cloves, crushed
5 cm/2 inch piece of fresh root ginger, peeled
   and grated
1 litre/1³/₄ pints Vegetable Stock
   (see page 9)
225 g/7¹/₂ oz baby spinach
plenty of freshly grated nutmeg
salt and pepper
croûtons, to serve

one Melt the butter with the oil in a large saucepan. Add the onion and fry for 5 minutes. Add the mushrooms and garlic and fry for 3 minutes.
two Stir in the ginger and stock. Bring to the boil, then reduce the heat, cover and simmer gently for 10 minutes.
three Add the spinach and nutmeg and simmer gently for 2 minutes. Season to taste with salt and pepper and serve scattered with croûtons.

creamed corn and potato soup

preparation time **5 mins**
cooking time **15 mins**
total time **20 mins** serves **4**

2 tablespoons olive oil
1 onion, chopped
2 celery sticks, thinly sliced
1 litre/1¾ pints Vegetable Stock (see page 9)
400 g/13 oz potatoes, diced
300 g/10 oz frozen sweetcorn
2 tablespoons chopped tarragon
plenty of freshly grated nutmeg
4 tablespoons double cream
salt and pepper

one Heat the oil in a large saucepan. Add the onion and celery and fry gently for 5 minutes. Add the stock and bring to the boil.
two Add the potatoes, reduce the heat and simmer, uncovered, for 5 minutes. Add the sweetcorn and tarragon, cover the pan and simmer for a further 5 minutes until the potatoes are tender.
three Transfer the soup to a food processor or blender and process until pulpy but not smooth, or leave the soup in the pan and use a hand-held electric blender.
four Return the soup to the pan, if necessary, and add the nutmeg and cream. Season to taste with salt and pepper and heat through gently for 1 minute before serving.

fresh ginger and parsnip soup

preparation time **5 mins**
cooking time **20 mins**
total time **25 mins** serves **4**

25 g/1 oz butter
50 g/2 oz fresh root ginger, peeled
  and thinly sliced
1 bunch of spring onions
500 g/1 lb parsnips, sliced
1 litre/1¾ pints Vegetable Stock
  (see page 9)
salt and pepper
crème fraîche, to serve

one Melt the butter in a saucepan, add the ginger and fry gently for 1 minute. Reserve 1 spring onion. Roughly chop the remainder and add to the pan with the parsnips. Fry gently for 2 minutes.

two Add the stock and bring to the boil. Reduce the heat, cover and simmer gently for 15 minutes until the parsnips are tender. Meanwhile, shred the reserved spring onion lengthways into fine ribbons.

three Transfer the soup to a food processor or blender and process until smooth, or leave the soup in the pan and use a hand-held electric blender.

four Return the soup to the pan, if necessary, season to taste with salt and pepper and heat through gently for 1 minute, then ladle into soup bowls. Serve topped with a spoonful of crème fraîche scattered with spring onion ribbons.

This is based on a Spanish soup in which the eggs are
poached or oven-baked in a rich, garlicky broth. Here,
pasta is added to give a little more substance to the dish.

garlic and paprika soup with a floating egg

preparation time **5 mins**
cooking time **15 mins**
total time **20 mins**   serves **4**

4 tablespoons olive oil
12 thick slices of baguette
5 garlic cloves, sliced
1 onion, finely chopped
1 tablespoon paprika
1 teaspoon ground cumin
good pinch of saffron threads
1.2 litres/2 pints Vegetable Stock
   (see page 9)
25 g/1 oz dried soup pasta
4 eggs
salt and pepper

one Heat the oil in a heavy-based saucepan. Add the bread and fry gently, turning once, until golden. Drain on kitchen paper.

two Add the garlic, onion, paprika and cumin to the pan and fry gently for 3 minutes. Add the saffron and stock and bring to the boil. Stir in the soup pasta. Reduce the heat, cover and simmer for about 8 minutes until the pasta is just tender. Season to taste with salt and pepper.

three Break the eggs on to a saucer and slide into the pan one at a time. Cook for about 2 minutes until poached.

four Stack 3 fried bread slices in each of 4 soup bowls. Ladle the soup over the bread, making sure each serving contains an egg. Serve immediately.

creamed shallot and rosemary soup

preparation time **10 mins**
cooking time **20 mins**
total time **30 mins**   serves **4**

4 tablespoons olive oil
375 g/12 oz shallots, sliced
1 red onion, roughly chopped
2 garlic cloves, roughly chopped
4 large rosemary sprigs
1 teaspoon caster sugar
750 ml/1¼ pints Vegetable Stock
   (see page 9)
5 tablespoons double cream
salt and pepper
toasted French bread croûtons, to serve

one Heat the oil in a saucepan. Add the shallots, onion, garlic, rosemary and sugar and fry gently for about 5 minutes until softened and lightly browned.

two Add the stock and bring to the boil. Reduce the heat, cover and simmer gently for about 15 minutes until the shallots and onion are tender.

three Transfer the soup to a food processor or blender and process until smooth, or leave the soup in the pan and use a hand-held electric blender.

four Return the soup to the pan, if necessary, stir in the cream and season to taste with salt and pepper. Heat through gently for 1 minute, ladle into soup bowls and serve sprinkled with croûtons.

pumpkin and coconut soup

preparation time **5 mins**
cooking time **12 mins**
total time **17 mins** serves **4**

3 tablespoons groundnut oil
4 thyme sprigs
2 garlic cloves, roughly chopped
1 red chilli, deseeded and roughly chopped
1 teaspoon cumin seeds
425 g/14 oz can solid-pack pumpkin
1 tablespoon dark muscovado sugar
450 ml/¾ pint Vegetable Stock
  (see page 9)
400 ml/14 fl oz can coconut milk
1–2 tablespoons lemon or lime juice
salt and pepper
roughly chopped coriander, to garnish

one Heat the oil in a saucepan. Strip the thyme leaves from the sprigs and add to the oil with the garlic, chilli and cumin seeds. Fry gently for 2 minutes.
two Add the pumpkin, sugar, stock and coconut milk and bring to the boil. Reduce the heat, cover and simmer gently for 10 minutes.
three Add the lemon or lime juice, season to taste with salt and pepper, then serve scattered with the chopped coriander.

chilli and pimiento soup

preparation time **10 mins**
cooking time **15 mins**
total time **25 mins** serves **4–6**

2 tablespoons olive oil
2 onions, chopped
2 garlic cloves, chopped
1 red chilli, deseeded and sliced
200 g/7 oz jar pimientos, drained
500 g/1 lb tomatoes, skinned
2 teaspoons caster sugar
1 litre/1¾ pints Vegetable Stock
  (see page 9)
2 tablespoons chopped coriander
4 tablespoons crème fraîche
salt and pepper

one Heat the oil in a large saucepan. Add the onions, garlic and chilli and fry gently for 3 minutes.
two Add the pimientos, tomatoes, sugar and stock and bring to the boil. Reduce the heat, cover and simmer gently for about 10 minutes until the tomatoes are soft.
three Transfer the soup to a food processor or blender and process until smooth, or leave the soup in the pan and use a hand-held electric blender.
four Return the soup to the pan, if necessary, and stir in the coriander and crème fraîche. Season to taste with salt and pepper and heat through gently for 1 minute before serving.

courgette and parmesan soup

preparation time **5 mins**
cooking time **15 mins**
total time **20 mins** serves **4**

25 g/1 oz butter
1 tablespoon olive oil
1 large onion, chopped
475 g/15 oz courgettes, sliced
75 g/3 oz pine nuts
1 tablespoon chopped sage
1 litre/1¾ pints Vegetable Stock
   (see page 9)
100 g/3½ oz Parmesan cheese, crumbled
4 tablespoons double cream
salt and pepper

one Melt the butter with the oil in a large saucepan. Add the onion, courgettes and pine nuts and fry gently for about 5 minutes until softened.

two Add the sage and stock and bring to the boil. Reduce the heat, cover and simmer gently for 5 minutes. Add the Parmesan cheese and cook for 2 minutes.

three Transfer the soup to a food processor or blender and process lightly until the ingredients are partially blended but not smooth, or leave the soup in the pan and use a hand-held electric blender.

four Return the soup to the pan, if necessary, and stir in the cream and a little salt and pepper. Heat through gently for 1 minute before serving.

pasta and noodles

The vast range of pasta and noodles available in supermarkets and specialist food shops is a bonus for all food lovers, particularly vegetarians. Opt for the more familiar Mediterranean approach with colourful vegetables and melting cheese or the exotic flavours of the East with egg noodle or rice noodle dishes.

cherry tomato and ricotta penne

preparation time **5 mins**
cooking time **10 mins**
total time **15 mins** serves **4**

300 g/10 oz dried penne
3 tablespoons olive oil
1 onion, chopped
4 garlic cloves, crushed
1 tablespoon chopped oregano
325 g/11 oz cherry tomatoes, halved
1 teaspoon caster sugar
3 tablespoons sun-dried tomato paste
250 g/8 oz ricotta cheese
salt and pepper

one Cook the pasta in plenty of lightly salted boiling water for about 10 minutes or until just tender.

two Meanwhile, heat the oil in a frying pan. Add the onion and fry gently for 3 minutes. Add the garlic, oregano, tomatoes and sugar and fry quickly for 1 minute, stirring. Add the sun-dried tomato paste and 6 tablespoons of water, season to taste with salt and pepper and bring to the boil. Place dessertspoonfuls of the ricotta cheese into the pan and heat through gently for 1 minute.

three Drain the pasta and pile on to serving plates. Spoon the tomato and cheese mixture on top, taking care not to break up the ricotta too much. Serve immediately.

ribbon pasta with aubergines and pine nuts

preparation time **5 mins**
cooking time **17 mins**
total time **22 mins** serves **4**

8 tablespoons olive oil
2 medium aubergines, diced
2 red onions, sliced
75 g/3 oz pine nuts
3 garlic cloves, crushed
5 tablespoons sun-dried tomato paste
150 ml/¼ pint Vegetable Stock
  (see page 9)
300 g/10 oz cracked pepper, tomato or
  mushroom-flavoured fresh ribbon pasta
100 g/3½ oz pitted black olives
salt and pepper
3 tablespoons roughly chopped flat leaf parsley,
  to garnish

one Heat the oil in a large frying pan or sauté pan and fry the aubergines and onions for 8–10 minutes until golden and tender. Add the pine nuts and garlic and fry for 2 minutes. Stir in the sun-dried tomato paste and stock and cook for 2 minutes.

two Meanwhile, cook the pasta in plenty of lightly salted boiling water for about 2 minutes or until just tender.

three Drain the pasta and return to the pan. Add the sauce and olives, season to taste with salt and pepper and toss together over a moderate heat for 1 minute until combined. Serve scattered with parsley.

pasta with watercress, dolcelatte and walnut sauce

preparation time **5 mins**
cooking time **5 mins**
total time **10 mins** serves **4**

300 g/10 oz fresh pasta shapes or
  dried pasta
75 g/3 oz walnut pieces, toasted
175 g/6 oz mature Dolcelatte, diced
finely grated rind of 1 lemon
200 g/7 oz crème fraîche
125 g/4 oz watercress sprigs, coarse stalks
  removed
salt and pepper

one Cook the fresh pasta in plenty of lightly salted boiling water for 2–3 minutes until just tender. Drain lightly and return to the pan with the residual water still clinging to the pasta. If you are using dried pasta, use the same amount and cook it while you prepare the other ingredients.

two Add the walnut pieces, cheese, lemon rind, crème fraîche, and watercress, and season to taste with salt and pepper.

three Toss the ingredients together over a low heat for 2 minutes until the crème fraîche has melted to make a sauce and the watercress has wilted. Serve immediately, with a tangy tomato and red onion salad, if liked.

ribbon pasta with tomatoes and tapenade

preparation time **10 mins**
cooking time **5 mins**
total time **15 mins** serves **4**

125 g/4 oz pitted black olives
1 red chilli, deseeded and sliced
4 tablespoons capers
2 tablespoons sun-dried tomato paste
3 tablespoons chopped basil
3 tablespoons chopped parsley or chervil
4 tomatoes, chopped
125 ml/4 fl oz olive oil
375 g/12 oz fresh ribbon pasta or fresh
  pasta shapes
salt and pepper
grated Parmesan cheese, to serve

one Place the olives, chilli and capers in a food processor or blender and process until quite finely chopped. Alternatively, finely chop them by hand. Mix with the sun-dried tomato paste, herbs, tomatoes and oil, and season to taste with salt and pepper.

two Cook the pasta in plenty of lightly salted boiling water for 2–3 minutes, or until it is only just tender. Drain and return to the saucepan.

three Add the olive mixture and toss the ingredients together lightly over a low heat for 2 minutes. Transfer to serving plates and serve sprinkled with Parmesan.

mushroom, courgette and mascarpone lasagne

preparation time **10 mins**
cooking time **20 mins**
total time **30 mins** serves **4**

25 g/1 oz dried porcini mushrooms
3 tablespoons olive oil
125 g/4 oz fresh lasagne sheets, halved
250 g/8 oz mascarpone
2 garlic cloves, crushed
3 tablespoons chopped dill or tarragon
25 g/1 oz butter
40 g/1½ oz breadcrumbs
500 g/1 lb cup mushrooms, sliced
2 courgettes, sliced
salt and pepper

one Place the dried mushrooms in a bowl, cover with boiling water and leave to stand while preparing the remaining ingredients.

two Bring a large saucepan of water to the boil with 1 tablespoon of the oil. Add the pasta sheets, one at a time, and cook for about 4 minutes until just tender. Drain.

three Meanwhile, mix together in a small bowl the mascarpone, garlic, dill or tarragon and season to taste with salt and pepper. Melt half the butter in a frying pan, add the breadcrumbs and fry gently for 2 minutes. Drain on kitchen paper.

four Melt the remaining butter in the pan with the remaining oil. Add the fresh mushrooms and courgettes and fry for about 6 minutes until golden. Drain the dried mushrooms, add to the pan and fry for 1 minute.

five Lay 4 pieces of lasagne, spaced slightly apart, in a shallow ovenproof dish. Spoon over a third of the vegetables, then a spoonful of the mascarpone mixture. Add another piece of lasagne to each stack and spoon over more vegetables and mascarpone. Finally, add the remaining lasagne, vegetables and mascarpone.

six Scatter with the fried breadcrumbs and bake in a preheated oven, 200°C (400°F), Gas Mark 6, for 6–8 minutes until heated through.

goats' cheese linguini with garlic and herb butter

preparation time **5 mins**
cooking time **7 mins**
total time **12 mins** serves **4**

300 g/10 oz firm goats' cheese
1 lemon
75 g/3 oz butter
2 tablespoons olive oil
3 shallots, finely chopped
2 garlic cloves, crushed
25 g/1 oz mixed chopped herbs, such as
    tarragon, chervil, parsley, dill
3 tablespoons capers
300 g/10 oz fresh linguini or
    250 g/8 oz dried linguini
salt and pepper

one Thickly slice the goats' cheese and
arrange on a lightly oiled, foil-lined grill rack.
Grill under a preheated hot grill for about
2 minutes until golden. Keep warm.
two Using a zester, pare rind strips from the
lemon, then squeeze the juice.
three Melt the butter in a frying pan or
sauté pan with the oil. Add the shallots and
garlic and fry gently for 3 minutes. Stir in the
herbs, capers and lemon juice, and season
to taste with salt and pepper.
four Cook the pasta in plenty of lightly
salted boiling water for about 2 minutes or
until just tender. Drain lightly and return to
the saucepan. Add the goats' cheese and
herb butter and toss the ingredients
together gently. Serve scattered with the
strips of lemon rind.

stir-fried vegetable noodles

preparation time **10 mins**
cooking time **12 mins**
total time **22 mins** serves **4**

250 g/8 oz medium egg noodles
4 tablespoons groundnut oil
1 bunch of spring onions, sliced
2 carrots, thinly sliced
2 garlic cloves, crushed
$1/4$ teaspoon dried chilli flakes
125 g/4 oz mangetout
125 g/4 oz shiitake mushrooms, halved
3 Chinese leaves, shredded
2 tablespoons light soy sauce
3 tablespoons hoisin sauce

one Cook the noodles in lightly salted boiling
water for about 4 minutes or until just
tender. Drain.
two Heat the oil in a large frying pan or
wok. Add the spring onions and carrots and
stir-fry for 3 minutes. Add the garlic, chilli
flakes, mangetout and mushrooms and stir-
fry for 2 minutes. Add the Chinese leaves
and stir-fry for 1 minute.
three Add the drained noodles to the pan
with the soy sauce and hoisin sauce. Stir-fry
over a gentle heat for 2 minutes until heated
through. Serve immediately.

If you cannot get fresh pasta for this dish, use dried and cook
it while you make the sauce. Always lightly drain pasta so that
it retains plenty of moisture and does not dry out the sauce.

A single Thai chilli gives this dish a really fiery kick.

Substitute a mild chilli if you are feeling cautious!

vegetable noodles in spiced coconut milk

preparation time **10 mins**
cooking time **10 mins**
total time **20 mins** serves **4**

125 g/4 oz dried medium egg noodles

2 tablespoons groundnut or vegetable oil

1 onion, chopped

1 Thai chilli, deseeded and sliced

3 garlic cloves, sliced

5 cm/2 inch piece of fresh root ginger, peeled and grated

2 teaspoons ground coriander

½ teaspoon ground turmeric

1 lemon grass stalk, finely sliced

400 ml/14 fl oz can coconut milk

300 ml/½ pint Vegetable Stock (see page 9)

125 g/4 oz spring greens or cabbage, finely shredded

275 g/9 oz runner beans or French beans, sliced diagonally

150 g/5 oz shiitake mushrooms, sliced

75 g/3 oz unsalted, shelled peanuts

salt and pepper

one Place the noodles in a bowl, cover with boiling water and leave to stand for 4 minutes.
two Heat the oil in a large saucepan. Add the onion, chilli, garlic, ginger, coriander, turmeric and lemon grass and fry gently for 5 minutes.
three Drain the noodles. Add the coconut milk and stock to the pan and bring just to the boil. Reduce the heat and stir in the spring greens or cabbage, beans, mushrooms and drained noodles. Cover and simmer for 5 minutes. Stir in the peanuts and season to taste with salt and pepper. Serve in deep bowls.

rice noodles with green beans and ginger

preparation time **10 mins**
cooking time **5 mins**
total time **15 mins** serves **4**

100 g/3½ oz fine rice noodles

125 g/4 oz green beans, halved

finely grated rind and juice of 2 limes

1 Thai chilli, deseeded and finely chopped

2.5 cm/1 inch piece of fresh root ginger, peeled and finely chopped

2 teaspoons caster sugar

small handful of coriander, chopped

50 g/2 oz dried pineapple pieces, chopped

one Place the noodles in a bowl, cover with plenty of boiling water and leave for 4 minutes until soft.
two Meanwhile, cook the beans in boiling water for about 3 minutes until tender. Drain.
three Mix together the lime rind and juice, chilli, ginger, caster sugar and coriander in a small bowl.
four Drain the noodles and place in a large serving bowl. Add the cooked beans, pineapple and dressing and toss together lightly before serving. To make a chilled alternative, refresh the noodles and beans under cold running water. To turn the dish into a main course for 2, stir in some diced smoked tofu.

rice noodle pancakes with stir-fried vegetables

preparation time **15 mins**
cooking time **15 mins**
total time **30 mins** serves **4**

175 g/6 oz dried wide rice noodles
1 green chilli, deseeded and sliced
2.5 cm/1 inch piece of fresh root ginger,
   peeled and grated
3 tablespoons chopped coriander
2 teaspoons plain flour
2 teaspoons oil, plus extra for shallow-frying

STIR-FRIED VEGETABLES
125 g/4 oz broccoli
2 tablespoons groundnut or vegetable oil
1 small onion, sliced
1 red pepper, cored, deseeded and sliced
1 yellow or orange pepper, cored, deseeded
   and sliced
125 g/4 oz sugarsnap peas, halved lengthways
6 tablespoons hoisin sauce
1 tablespoon lime juice
salt and pepper

one Cook the noodles in lightly salted boiling water for 3 minutes or until tender. Drain well. Transfer to a bowl, then add the chilli, ginger, coriander, flour and the 2 teaspoons of oil and mix well. Set aside.

two Thinly slice the broccoli stalks and cut the florets into small pieces. Cook the stalks in boiling water for 30 seconds, add the florets and cook for a further 30 seconds. Drain the broccoli well.

three Heat the groundnut or vegetable oil in a wok or large frying pan, add the onion and stir-fry for 2 minutes. Add the peppers and stir-fry for 3 minutes until softened but still retaining texture. Stir in the cooked broccoli, sugarsnap peas, hoisin sauce and lime juice, season to taste with salt and pepper and set aside.

four Heat some oil in a frying pan to a depth of 1 cm/½ inch. Place 4 large separate spoonfuls of the noodles (half the mixture) in the oil. Fry for about 5 minutes until crisp and lightly coloured. Drain the pancakes on kitchen paper. Keep warm while cooking the remaining noodle mixture.

five Heat the vegetables through for 1 minute in the wok or frying pan. Place 2 pancakes on each of 4 serving plates and pile the stir-fried vegetables on top.

beans and pulses

Simply opening a can of beans, lentils or other pulses provides the vegetarian cook with one of the most versatile vehicles for quick and easy main meals. Use them purely as a base ingredient, letting the highly flavoured additions of garlic, spices, herbs and aromatics transform them into culinary delights.

nut koftas with minted yogurt

preparation time **15 mins**
cooking time **10 mins**
total time **25 mins** serves **4**

5–6 tablespoons groundnut or
   vegetable oil
1 onion, chopped
½ teaspoon crushed chilli flakes
2 garlic cloves, roughly chopped
1 tablespoon medium curry paste
425 g/14 oz can borlotti or cannellini beans,
   rinsed and drained
125 g/4 oz ground almonds
75 g/3 oz chopped honey-roast
   or salted almonds
1 small egg
200 ml/7 fl oz Greek yogurt
2 tablespoons chopped mint
1 tablespoon lemon juice
salt and pepper
warm naan bread, to serve
mint sprigs, to garnish

one Soak 8 bamboo skewers in hot water while preparing the koftas. Alternatively, use metal skewers which do not require pre-soaking. Heat 3 tablespoons of the oil in a frying pan, add the onion and fry for 4 minutes. Add the chilli flakes, garlic and curry paste and fry for 1 minute.

two Transfer to a food processor or blender with the beans, ground almonds, chopped almonds, egg and a little salt and pepper and process until the mixture starts to bind together.

three Using lightly floured hands, take about one-eighth of the mixture and mould around a skewer, forming it into a sausage about 2.5 cm/1 inch thick. Make 7 more koftas in the same way.

four Place on a foil-lined grill rack and brush with a further 1 tablespoon of the oil. Grill under a preheated moderate grill for about 5 minutes, until golden, turning once.

five Meanwhile, mix together the yogurt and mint in a small serving bowl and season to taste with salt and pepper. In a separate bowl, mix together the remaining oil, lemon juice and a little salt and pepper.

six Brush the koftas with the lemon dressing and serve with the yogurt dressing on warm naan bread garnished with mint sprigs.

braised lentils with mushrooms and gremolata

preparation time **5 mins**
cooking time **25 mins**
total time **30 mins** serves **4**

50 g/2 oz butter
1 onion, chopped
2 celery sticks, sliced
2 carrots, sliced
175 g/6 oz Puy lentils, rinsed
600 ml/1 pint Vegetable Stock (see page 9)
250 ml/8 fl oz dry white wine
2 bay leaves
2 tablespoons chopped thyme
3 tablespoons extra virgin olive oil
325 g/11 oz mushrooms, sliced
salt and pepper

GREMOLATA
2 tablespoons chopped parsley
finely grated rind of 1 lemon
2 garlic cloves, chopped

one Melt the butter in a saucepan and fry the onion, celery and carrots for 3 minutes. Add the lentils, stock, wine, herbs and a little salt and pepper. Bring to the boil, then reduce the heat and simmer gently, uncovered, for about 20 minutes or until the lentils are tender.
two Meanwhile, mix together the ingredients for the gremolata.
three Heat the oil in a frying pan. Add the mushrooms and fry for about 2 minutes until golden. Season lightly with salt and pepper.
four Ladle the lentils on to serving plates, top with the mushrooms and serve scattered with the gremolata.

black bean and cabbage stew

preparation time **8 mins**
cooking time **20 mins**
total time **28 mins** serves **4**

4 tablespoons olive oil
1 large onion, chopped
1 leek, chopped
3 garlic cloves, sliced
1 tablespoon paprika
2 tablespoons chopped marjoram or thyme
625 g/1¼ lb potatoes, cut into small chunks
425 g/14 oz can black beans or black-eyed beans, rinsed and drained
1 litre/1¾ pints Vegetable Stock (see page 9)
175 g/6 oz cabbage or spring greens, shredded
salt and pepper
chunky bread, to serve

one Heat the oil in a large saucepan. Add the onion and leek and fry gently for 3 minutes. Add the garlic and paprika and fry for 2 minutes.
two Add the marjoram or thyme, potatoes, beans and stock and bring to the boil. Reduce the heat, cover and simmer gently for about 10 minutes until the potatoes have softened but are not mushy.
three Add the cabbage or spring greens and season to taste with salt and pepper. Simmer for a further 5 minutes. Serve the stew with chunky bread.

red lentil dhal with okra

preparation time **5 mins**
cooking time **25 mins**
total time **30 mins** serves **4**

1 onion, chopped
250 g/8 oz red split lentils, rinsed and drained
1 teaspoon ground turmeric
1 green chilli, deseeded and sliced
2 tablespoons tomato purée
900 ml/1½ pints Vegetable Stock (see page 9)
25 g/1 oz creamed coconut
2 tablespoons groundnut or vegetable oil
250 g/8 oz okra, trimmed and halved
   crossways
2 teaspoons cumin seeds
1 tablespoon mustard seeds
2 teaspoons black onion seeds
2 garlic cloves, chopped
6 curry leaves (optional)
salt and pepper

one Place the onion, lentils, turmeric, chilli, tomato purée, stock and creamed coconut in a saucepan. Bring to the boil, then reduce the heat and simmer gently, uncovered, for 15 minutes until the mixture is thickened and pulpy, stirring frequently.

two Meanwhile, heat the oil in a frying pan. Add the okra, cumin seeds, mustard seeds, black onion seeds, garlic and curry leaves, if using, and fry gently for about 5 minutes until the okra is tender.

three Season the lentil dhal to taste with salt and pepper and spoon on to serving plates. Serve topped with the spiced okra.

Red lentils cook much faster than many pulses and do not need pre-soaking, making them a perfect choice for quick and easy cooking. Serve this spicy dish with naan or paratha bread and mango chutney to complete the meal.

chickpea purée with eggs and spiced oil

preparation time **5 mins**
cooking time **7 mins**
total time **12 mins** serves **2**

400 g/13 oz can chickpeas, rinsed
    and drained
3 garlic cloves, sliced
4 tablespoons tahini
4 tablespoons milk
5 tablespoons olive oil
4 teaspoons lemon juice
2 eggs
½ teaspoon each of cumin, coriander
    and fennel seeds, lightly crushed
1 teaspoon sesame seeds
¼ teaspoon chilli flakes
good pinch of ground turmeric
salt and pepper
coriander leaves, to garnish

one Place the chickpeas in a food processor or blender with the garlic, tahini, milk, 2 tablespoons of the oil and 3 teaspoons of the lemon juice. Season to taste with salt and pepper and process until smooth, scraping the mixture from around the sides of the bowl halfway through. Transfer to a small heavy-based saucepan and heat through gently for about 3 minutes while preparing the eggs.

two Heat another tablespoon of the oil in a small frying pan and fry the eggs. Pile the chickpea purée on to serving plates and top each mound with an egg.

three Add the remaining oil and spices to the pan and heat through gently for 1 minute. Season lightly with salt and pepper and stir in the remaining lemon juice. Pour over the eggs and serve garnished with coriander leaves.

Smooth chickpea purée, topped with fried eggs and
spicy oil, makes a great snack at any time of the day.
Serve any leftover purée just as you would hummus,
with warm pitta bread.

cannellini beans on toast

Preparation time **5 mins**
cooking time **25 mins**
total time **30 mins** serves **2–3**

2 tablespoons groundnut or vegetable oil
1 onion, chopped
1 celery stick, thinly sliced
1 teaspoon cornflour
425 g/14 oz can cannellini beans
250 g/8 oz canned chopped tomatoes
300 ml/½ pint Vegetable Stock
  (see page 9)
1 tablespoon coarse-grain mustard
1 tablespoon black treacle
1 tablespoon tomato ketchup
1 tablespoon Worcestershire sauce
salt and pepper
toasted chunky bread, to serve

one Heat the oil in a saucepan and fry the onion and celery for 5 minutes until golden. Blend the cornflour with 2 tablespoons water and add to the pan with the remaining ingredients.
two Bring to the boil, reduce the heat slightly and cook, uncovered, for about 20 minutes, stirring frequently, until the mixture is thickened and pulpy. Pile on toast to serve.

red beans with coconut and cashews

preparation time **8 mins**
cooking time **22 mins**
total time **30 mins** serves **4**

3 tablespoons groundnut or vegetable oil
2 onions, chopped
2 small carrots, thinly sliced
3 garlic cloves, crushed
1 red pepper, cored, deseeded and chopped
2 bay leaves
1 tablespoon paprika
3 tablespoons tomato purée
400 ml/14 fl oz can coconut milk
200 g/7 oz canned chopped tomatoes
150 ml/¼ pint Vegetable Stock (see page 9)
425 g/14 oz can red kidney beans, rinsed
  and drained
100 g/3½ oz unsalted, shelled cashew
  nuts, toasted
small handful of coriander, roughly chopped
salt and pepper
boiled black or white rice, to serve

one Heat the oil in a large saucepan. Add the onions and carrots and fry for 3 minutes. Add the garlic, pepper and bay leaves and fry for 5 minutes until the vegetables are soft and well browned.
two Stir in the paprika, tomato purée, coconut milk, tomatoes, stock and beans and bring to the boil. Reduce the heat and simmer, uncovered, for 12 minutes until the vegetables are tender.
three Stir in the cashew nuts and coriander, season to taste with salt and pepper and heat through for 2 minutes. Serve with rice.

chilli cheese and corn cakes

preparation time **15 mins**
cooking time **6 mins**
total time **21 mins** serves **4**

125 g/4 oz frozen sweetcorn, thawed
200 g/7 oz can butter beans, rinsed
125 g/4 oz semolina or polenta
125 g/4 oz Cheddar cheese, grated
½ teaspoon dried chilli flakes
4 tablespoons mango chutney
1 egg
oil, for shallow-frying
salt and pepper

one Place the sweetcorn and beans in a food processor or blender and process until chopped into very small pieces, or mash with a fork in a bowl. Transfer to a bowl, if necessary, and add the semolina or polenta, cheese and chilli flakes.
two Chop any large pieces of chutney. Add to the bowl with the egg and mix to a dough. Season with salt and pepper.
three Using lightly floured hands, shape the mixture into 12 balls, then flatten into cakes. Heat a little oil in a frying pan, add the cakes and fry gently for about 3 minutes on each side until golden. Drain and serve warm.

bean and beer casserole with baby dumplings

preparation time **5 mins**
cooking time **25 mins**
total time **30 mins** serves **4**

4 tablespoons groundnut or vegetable oil
1 onion, sliced
1 celery stick, thinly sliced
1 parsnip, sliced
425 g/14 oz can mixed beans,
   rinsed and drained
425 g/14 oz can baked beans
250 ml/8 fl oz Guinness or stout
250 ml/8 fl oz Vegetable Stock (see page 9)
4 tablespoons roughly chopped herbs, such
   as rosemary, marjoram, thyme
150 g/5 oz self-raising flour
75 g/3 oz vegetable suet
2 tablespoons coarse-grain mustard
salt and pepper

one Heat the oil in a large saucepan or flameproof casserole and fry the onion, celery and parsnip for 3 minutes. Add the mixed beans, baked beans, beer, stock and 3 tablespoons of the herbs. Bring to the boil and let the mixture bubble, uncovered, for 8–10 minutes until slightly thickened.
two Meanwhile, mix the flour, suet, mustard, remaining herbs and a little salt and pepper in a bowl with 8–9 tablespoons cold water to make a soft dough.
three Evenly distribute 8 spoonfuls of the dough in the casserole and cover with a lid. Cook for a further 10 minutes until the dumplings are light and fluffy. Serve immediately.

red bean and pepper cakes with lemon mayonnaise

preparation time **10 mins**
cooking time **10 mins**
total time **20 mins** serves **4**

75 g/3 oz French beans, roughly chopped
2 tablespoons groundnut or vegetable oil
1 red pepper, cored, deseeded and diced
4 garlic cloves, crushed
2 teaspoons mild chilli powder
425 g/14 oz can red kidney beans,
    rinsed and drained
75 g/3 oz fresh white breadcrumbs
1 egg yolk
oil, for shallow-frying
salt and pepper

LEMON MAYONNAISE
4 tablespoons mayonnaise
finely grated rind of 1 lemon
1 teaspoon lemon juice

one Blanch the French beans in boiling water for 1–2 minutes until softened. Drain.
two Meanwhile, heat the groundnut or vegetable oil in a frying pan, add the red pepper, garlic and chilli powder and fry for 2 minutes.
three Transfer the mixture to a food processor or blender and add the red kidney beans, breadcrumbs and egg yolk. Process very briefly until the ingredients are coarsely chopped. Add the drained French beans and season to taste with salt and pepper and process, again very briefly, until the ingredients are just combined.
four Turn the mixture into a bowl and divide into 8 portions. Using lightly floured hands, shape the portions into little cakes.
five Mix the mayonnaise with the lemon rind and juice, and season to taste with salt and pepper.
six Heat the oil for shallow-frying in a large frying pan and fry the cakes for about 3 minutes on each side until crisp and golden. Serve with the lemon mayonnaise.

Pack these crisp bean cakes into warm pitta bread and serve with salad for a fairly substantial lunch or supper dish. Any unbaked cakes will keep in the refrigerator, interleaved with greaseproof paper, for a day or so.

rice

Rice is the staple ingredient of so many countries worldwide that it offers a fabulous choice of interesting dishes for the vegetarian cook. Although some varieties take longer to cook, there are still plenty of easy options on offer, including sweet, aromatic oriental dishes, spicy Middle Eastern-style pilafs and creamy, comforting Italian risottos.

chestnut risotto cakes

preparation time **10 mins**
cooking time **20 mins**
total time **30 mins** serves **4**

15 g/½ oz dried porcini mushrooms
1 tablespoon olive oil
175 g/6 oz risotto rice
600 ml/1 pint hot Vegetable Stock
  (see page 9)
50 g/2 oz butter
1 onion, chopped
3 garlic cloves, crushed
200 g/7 oz cooked, peeled chestnuts
75 g/3 oz Parmesan cheese, grated
1 egg, lightly beaten
50 g/2 oz polenta
oil, for shallow-frying
salt and pepper

one Place the dried mushrooms in a bowl and cover with boiling water. Leave to stand.
two Heat the olive oil in a saucepan and cook the rice, stirring, for 1 minute. Add the hot stock and bring to the boil. Reduce the heat, partially cover and simmer for 12–15 minutes, stirring frequently, until the rice is tender and the stock is absorbed. Transfer to a bowl.
three Meanwhile, melt the butter in a saucepan. Add the onion and garlic and fry gently for 2 minutes. Drain and chop the mushrooms, then add to the rice with the onion mixture, chopped chestnuts, Parmesan and egg. Stir until combined and season lightly with salt and pepper.
four Divide into 12 portions, pat each into a cake and coat in the polenta. Heat the oil for shallow-frying and fry the cakes for 2 minutes on each side until golden. Serve immediately.

broad bean, lemon and parmesan risotto

preparation time **5 mins**
cooking time **25 mins**
total time **30 mins** serves **4**

25 g/1 oz butter
2 tablespoons olive oil
1 onion, chopped
2 garlic cloves, crushed
400 g/13 oz risotto rice
150 ml/¼ pint dry white wine
1.2 litres/2 pints hot Vegetable Stock
  (see page 9)
150 g/5 oz fresh or frozen broad beans
50 g/2 oz Parmesan cheese, grated, plus
  extra to serve
finely grated rind and juice of 1 lemon
salt and pepper

one Melt the butter with the oil in a large, heavy-based saucepan. Add the onion and garlic and fry gently for 3 minutes. Add the rice and cook for 1 minute, stirring.
two Add the wine and cook, stirring, until the wine is absorbed. Add a little stock and cook, stirring, until almost absorbed. Continue in the same way, gradually adding more stock, until half the stock is used. Stir in the beans.
three Gradually add the remaining stock until the mixture is thickened and creamy but still retaining a little bite. This will take 15–18 minutes. Stir in the Parmesan, lemon rind and juice, and season to taste with salt and pepper. Turn on to serving plates and serve with extra Parmesan cheese.

red rice and pepper pilaf

preparation time **5 mins**
cooking time **25 mins**
total time **30 mins** serves **4**

275 g/9 oz Camargue red rice
600 ml/1 pint hot Vegetable Stock (see page 9)
3 tablespoons olive oil
1 large red onion, chopped
2 tablespoons paprika
3 garlic cloves, crushed
1 teaspoon saffron threads
2 red peppers, cored, deseeded and sliced
finely grated rind of 1 lemon,
2 teaspoons lemon juice
4 tomatoes, roughly chopped
small handful of flat leaf parsley, roughly
   chopped, plus extra to garnish
50 g/2 oz pitted black olives
salt and pepper

one Put the rice, hot stock and 600 ml/ 1 pint boiling water in a large saucepan. Bring to the boil, cover and cook for 25 minutes until tender, stirring frequently.
two Meanwhile, heat the oil in a saucepan or sauté pan. Add the onion and fry gently for 3 minutes. Add the paprika, garlic, saffron and peppers and fry gently for 5 minutes.
three Stir in the lemon rind and juice, tomatoes and parsley and cook gently, uncovered, for 5 minutes.
four Drain the rice and add to the pan with the olives and season to taste with salt and pepper. Toss together and serve scattered with extra parsley.

japanese rice with nori

preparation time **10 mins**
cooking time **15 mins**
total time **25 mins** serves **4**

225 g/7½ oz Japanese sushi or
    glutinous rice
2 tablespoons black or white sesame seeds
1 teaspoon coarse salt
1 tablespoon groundnut or vegetable oil
2 eggs, beaten
4 spring onions, finely sliced
1 red chilli, deseeded and sliced
4 tablespoons seasoned rice vinegar
2 teaspoons caster sugar
1 tablespoon light soy sauce
25 g/1 oz pickled Japanese ginger
2 sheets of roasted nori seaweed

one Place the rice in a heavy-based saucepan with 400 ml/14 fl oz water. Bring to the boil, then reduce the heat and simmer, uncovered, for about 5 minutes until all the water is absorbed. Cover the pan and cook for a further 5 minutes until the rice is cooked.

two Meanwhile, place the sesame seeds in a small frying pan with the salt and heat gently for about 2 minutes until the seeds are lightly toasted. Remove from the pan and set aside.

three Heat the oil in the pan, add the beaten eggs and cook gently until just firm. Slide the omelette on to a plate, roll up and cut across into shreds.

four Transfer the cooked rice to a bowl and stir in the spring onions, chilli, rice vinegar, sugar, soy sauce, ginger and half the toasted sesame seeds. Crumble 1 sheet of nori over the rice and stir in with the omelette shreds.

five Transfer to a serving dish. Crumble the remaining nori over the rice and scatter with the remaining toasted sesame seeds.

spiced pilaf with pickled walnuts

preparation time **7 mins**
cooking time **23 mins**
total time **30 mins** serves **4**

3 tablespoons olive oil
1 large onion, chopped
4 garlic cloves, sliced
¼ teaspoon ground allspice
50 g/2 oz pine nuts
2 teaspoons ground ginger
250 g/8 oz long-grain rice
1 teaspoon saffron threads
300 ml/½ pint Vegetable Stock
  (see page 9)
50 g/2 oz pickled walnuts, roughly chopped
50 g/2 oz ready-to-eat dried apricots, sliced
4 tablespoons roughly chopped coriander
salt and pepper
Greek yogurt, to serve

one Heat the oil in a large, heavy-based
frying pan or sauté pan. Add the onion,
garlic, allspice, pine nuts and ginger and fry
gently for 5 minutes.
two Add the rice and cook for 1 minute,
stirring. Add the saffron and stock and bring
to the boil. Reduce the heat, partially cover
and simmer gently for 10–15 minutes until
the rice is tender, adding a little more stock
if the mixture becomes too dry.
three Add the pickled walnuts, apricots and
coriander, and season to taste with salt and
pepper. Heat through for 2 minutes, then
serve with Greek yogurt.

sage and walnut risotto with a cheese crust

preparation time **5 mins**
cooking time **25 mins**
total time **30 mins** serves **4**

50 g/2 oz butter
1 onion, chopped
375 g/12 oz risotto rice
1.3 litres/2¼ pints hot Vegetable Stock
  (see page 9)
2 tablespoons chopped sage
50 g/2 oz walnuts, roughly chopped
250 g/8 oz Brie, thinly sliced
salt and pepper
leafy salad, to serve

one Melt the butter in a large, heavy-based
saucepan. Add the onion and fry for 2 minutes.
Add the rice and fry for 1 minute, stirring.
two Add 2 ladlefuls of the stock and cook,
stirring, until almost absorbed. Add a little
more stock and continue cooking, stirring,
until almost absorbed. Continue in the same
way until all the stock is used and the rice is
creamy but still retaining a little bite. This
will take 15–18 minutes.
three Stir in the sage and walnuts, and
season to taste with salt and pepper.
Transfer to a shallow flameproof serving dish
and cover with the slices of Brie. Cook
under a preheated hot grill for about
3 minutes until the cheese has melted.
Serve with a leafy salad.

kedgeree with artichokes and rosemary butter

preparation time **5 mins**
cooking time **15 mins**
total time **20 mins** serves **4**

250 g/8 oz basmati rice
50 g/2 oz butter, melted
1 tablespoon chopped rosemary
1 tablespoon chopped chives
1 tablespoon lime juice
2 tablespoons olive oil
1 onion, chopped
1 teaspoon coriander seeds, crushed
1 teaspoon fennel seeds, crushed
425 g/14 oz can artichoke hearts, rinsed,
    drained and halved
6 hard-boiled eggs, cut into wedges
salt and pepper
lime wedges, to garnish

one Cook the rice in plenty of lightly salted boiling water for about 10 minutes or until it is just tender. Drain well.

two Meanwhile, mix together the melted butter, chopped herbs and lime juice, and season with salt and pepper.

three Heat the oil in a frying pan. Add the onion and spices and fry gently for 5 minutes. Add the rice to the pan with the artichoke hearts, season to taste with salt and pepper and heat through gently for 1 minute. Lightly stir in the eggs.

four Transfer to serving plates and pour over the herb butter. Serve garnished with lime wedges.

Cooking food in banana-leaf parcels keeps its flavour and moisture intact and makes an exotic presentation if you are entertaining. If not, simply wrap the rice in nonstick baking paper or foil for heating through.

coconut rice with peanut sauce

preparation time **15 mins**
cooking time **12 mins**
total time **27 mins** serves **4**

300 g/10 oz jasmine or Thai fragrant rice
75 g/3 oz creamed coconut
$\frac{1}{2}$ teaspoon dried chilli flakes
1 teaspoon caster sugar
small handful of coriander, chopped
4 x 28 cm/11 inch lengths of banana leaf,
   washed
1 lime
1 papaya, peeled, deseeded and sliced
4 spring onions, shredded lengthways
75 g/3 oz roasted, salted cashew nuts
salt and pepper

SAUCE
½ small onion, finely chopped
1 lemon grass stalk, finely sliced
4 tablespoons peanut butter
1 tablespoon dark muscovado sugar
25 g/1 oz creamed coconut
2 tablespoons soy sauce

one Place the rice in a saucepan with the creamed coconut and 350 ml/12 fl oz water. Bring to the boil, then reduce the heat and simmer gently, stirring frequently, for about 5 minutes until the water is almost absorbed and the mixture is creamy. Remove the pan from the heat and stir in the chilli flakes, caster sugar and coriander. Season to taste with salt and pepper.

two Spoon the mixture on to the centres of the banana leaves. Fold over the sides to enclose the rice, then tuck the ends under to form parcels. Place on a baking sheet and bake in a preheated oven, 220°C (425°F), Gas Mark 7, for about 5 minutes until the leaves have browned.

three Meanwhile, place the ingredients for the sauce in a small saucepan and heat through gently until thickened, stirring the mixture frequently.

four Using a canelle knife, pare fine strips of rind from the lime. Cut away the remaining white skin and discard, then cut between the membranes to remove the segments.

five Open the parcels and add the papaya, spring onions, cashew nuts, lime segments and rind. Serve with the sauce.

lemon rice with feta and chargrilled peppers

preparation time **5 mins**
cooking time **25 mins**
total time **30 mins** serves **4**

3 tablespoons olive oil
1 onion, sliced
3 garlic cloves, crushed
1 small lemon, sliced
325 g/11 oz long-grain rice
600 ml/1 pint Vegetable Stock (see page 9)
1 tablespoon chopped rosemary
1 large courgette
2 red peppers, cored, deseeded and cut into 8
1 yellow pepper, cored, deseeded and cut
   into 8
200 g/7 oz feta cheese, diced
salt and pepper

one Heat 2 tablespoons of the oil in a saucepan. Add the onion and fry for 3 minutes. Add the garlic and lemon slices and fry for 2 minutes. Add the rice, stock and rosemary and bring to the boil. Reduce the heat slightly, partially cover and cook for about 15 minutes until the rice is just tender and the stock is absorbed.

two Cut the courgette diagonally into long thin slices. Heat the remaining oil in a large frying pan. Add the courgette slices and peppers and cook for 5 minutes until coloured, turning the vegetables and pressing the peppers down on to the pan with a fish slice as they soften.

three Add the cooked vegetables to the rice, fold in gently with the feta and season to taste with salt and pepper. Heat through for 1 minute before serving.

beetroot risotto with horseradish and mixed leaves

preparation time **5 mins**
cooking time **25 mins**
total time **30 mins** serves **4**

4 tablespoons olive oil
1 large red onion, chopped
3 garlic cloves, crushed
400 g/13 oz risotto rice
1.3 litres/2¼ pints hot Vegetable
   Stock (see page 9)
425 g/14 oz cooked beetroot, finely diced
4 tablespoons roughly chopped dill
1–2 tablespoons freshly grated horseradish or
   1 tablespoon hot horseradish from a jar
50 g/2 oz salted macadamia nuts or almonds
salt and pepper
mixed salad leaves, to serve

one Heat the oil in a large, heavy-based saucepan. Add the onion and garlic and fry gently for 3 minutes. Add the rice and cook for 1 minute, stirring.

two Add 2 ladlefuls of the hot stock and cook, stirring frequently, until almost absorbed. Continue in the same way until all the stock is used and the rice is creamy but still retaining a little bite. This will take about 20 minutes.

three Stir in the beetroot, dill, horseradish and nuts. Season to taste with salt and pepper and heat through gently for 1 minute. Spoon the risotto on to plates and serve with mixed salad leaves.

This risotto makes an impressive main course for 4 people, but will also serve 6–8 as a colourful starter. If you can find fresh horseradish, use it in place of the bottled variety. The flavour is far superior, but beware of its heat intensity which can be anything from harmlessly mild to hot and fiery, depending on its freshness.

pizza and bread

Made using a quick and simple bread base, lavishly topped pizzas are surprisingly quick to prepare and create an enduringly appealing lunch or supper dish. Ready-made breads, both yeast-risen and flat, offer ultra-easy meal solutions, providing instant bases for a variety of exciting vegetarian fillings and toppings.

spinach, onion and cream cheese pizza

preparation time **12 mins**
cooking time **15 mins**
total time **27 mins** serves **4**

250 g/8 oz self-raising flour
3 tablespoons olive oil
1 teaspoon salt

TOPPING
100 g/3½ oz full-fat soft cheese
100 g/3½ oz crème fraîche
2 teaspoons chopped rosemary
3 tablespoons olive oil
1 large onion, finely sliced
375 g/12 oz young spinach
salt and pepper

one Grease a large baking sheet. Place the flour in a bowl with the oil and salt. Add 100 ml/3½ fl oz water and mix to a soft dough, adding a little more water, a teaspoonful at a time, if the dough is too dry. Roll out on a floured surface into a round about 28 cm/11 inches in diameter. Place the round on the prepared baking sheet and bake in a preheated oven, 230°C (450°F), Gas Mark 8, for 5 minutes until a crust has formed.

two For the topping, beat together the cream cheese, crème fraîche, rosemary and a little salt and pepper.

three Heat the oil in a frying pan and fry the onion for 3–4 minutes until softened. Add the spinach and a little salt and pepper and cook, stirring, for about 1 minute until the spinach has just wilted.

four Pile the spinach on to the pizza base, spreading to within 1 cm/½ inch of the edge. Place spoonfuls of the cheese mixture over the spinach. Bake for a further 8 minutes or until turning golden.

spinach and egg muffins with mustard hollandaise

preparation time **10 mins**
cooking time **8 mins**
total time **18 mins** serves **4**

200 g/7 oz baby spinach
plenty of freshly ground nutmeg
1 tablespoon lemon juice
2 egg yolks
1 tablespoon coarse-grain mustard
75 g/3 oz lightly salted butter, diced
4 muffins, split
1 tablespoon vinegar
4 eggs

one Place the spinach and nutmeg in a saucepan and add 1 tablespoon water. Set aside while making the sauce.
two Place the lemon juice, egg yolks and mustard in a heatproof bowl over a pan of gently simmering water. Whisk in the butter, a piece at a time, until the sauce is thickened and smooth. This takes about 5 minutes. If the sauce becomes too thick, whisk in a tablespoonful of hot water. Keep the sauce over the simmering water until ready to use.
three Toast the muffins and keep warm. Place the vinegar in a saucepan with plenty of hot water, bring to the boil and poach the eggs. Cover the spinach pan with a lid and cook for about 1 minute until the spinach has wilted.
four Transfer the muffins to serving plates, pile them up with the spinach, followed by the poached eggs and finally the sauce. Serve immediately.

goats' cheese, onion and pine nut bruschetta

preparation time **5 mins**
cooking time **10 mins**
total time **15 mins** serves **2**

5 tablespoons olive oil
1 small red onion, chopped
3 tablespoons pine nuts
4 slices ciabatta bread
1 garlic clove, crushed
2 tablespoons chopped flat leaf parsley
150 g/5 oz firm goats' cheese, thinly sliced

one Heat 2 tablespoons of the oil in a frying pan, add the onion and pine nuts and fry for 3 minutes until softened.
two Toast one side of the bread under a preheated moderate grill until golden. Mix together the garlic, parsley and remaining oil in a bowl. Turn the bread over and spread with the garlic mixture. Grill until pale golden.
three Lay the goats' cheese and onion mixture over the toast, increase the heat and grill for a further 2 minutes. Serve warm.

tomato, artichoke and mozzarella pizza

preparation time **10 mins**
cooking time **20 mins**
total time **30 mins** serves **4**

250 g/8 oz self-raising flour
3 tablespoons oil
1 teaspoon salt
2 tablespoons sun-dried tomato paste

TOPPING
1 tablespoon sun-dried tomato paste
2 large, mild red or green chillies, halved
   and deseeded
3 tablespoons chopped mixed herbs, such
   as parsley, oregano, rosemary, chives
50 g/2 oz sun-dried tomatoes in oil, drained
   and sliced
150 g/5 oz baby artichokes in oil, drained
2 plum tomatoes, cut into quarters
150 g/5 oz mozzarella cheese, sliced
50 g/2 oz black olives
salt and pepper

one Grease a large baking sheet. Place the flour in a bowl with the oil, salt and sun-dried tomato paste. Add 100 ml/3½ fl oz water and mix to a soft dough, adding a little more water if necessary.
two Roll out the dough on a lightly floured surface to a round about 28 cm/11 inches in diameter. Place on the prepared baking sheet and bake in a preheated oven, 230°C (450°F), Gas Mark 8, for 5 minutes.
three For the topping, spread the pizza base to within 1 cm/½ inch of the edge with the sun-dried tomato paste. Cut the chillies in half lengthways again and scatter over the pizza with half the herbs, the sun-dried tomatoes, artichokes, tomatoes, cheese and olives. Scatter the remaining herbs on top and season lightly with salt and pepper. Return to the oven and bake for 10–15 minutes until the cheese has melted and the vegetables are beginning to colour.

Homemade pizzas look and taste infinitely better than most store-bought
ones and are certainly much better value for money. If you are unable to
find the large, really mild chillies, use strips of red pepper instead or
scatter the pizza with a finely sliced hot chilli.

tortilla wraps with refried beans and coriander relish

preparation time **5 mins**
cooking time **5 mins**
total time **10 mins** serves **2**

250 g/8 oz can refried beans
2 tablespoons chilli sauce
2 red peppers, cored, deseeded and
  finely chopped
4 spring onions, finely sliced
1 teaspoon cumin seeds
finely grated rind and juice of 1 lime
1 teaspoon caster sugar
15 g/½ oz coriander, chopped
4 tortillas
salt and pepper

one Place the beans in a small saucepan
with the chilli sauce and heat through gently
for 3 minutes.
two Mix together in a bowl the peppers,
spring onions, cumin seeds, lime rind and
juice, sugar and coriander. Season to taste
with salt and pepper.
three Lightly toast the tortillas and spread
with the refried beans. Spoon over the
coriander mixture and roll up the tortillas.

cheddar burgers with cucumber salsa

preparation time **10 mins**
cooking time **8 mins**
total time **18 mins** serves **4**

200 g/7 oz can butter beans, rinsed
1 onion, finely chopped
1 carrot, grated
100 g/3½ oz mature Cheddar cheese, grated
100 g/3½ oz breadcrumbs
1 egg
1 teaspoon cumin seeds
oil, for shallow-frying
4 round French rolls
salt and pepper
salad, to serve

SALSA
½ small cucumber
2 tablespoons chopped coriander
2 spring onions, finely chopped
1 tablespoon lemon or lime juice
1 teaspoon caster sugar

one Place the butter beans in a bowl and
lightly mash with a fork. Add the onion,
carrot, cheese, breadcrumbs, egg, cumin
seeds and salt and pepper and mix until
evenly combined.
two Shape the mixture into 4 small flat
cakes. Heat a little oil in a large frying pan
and fry the burgers for about 8 minutes,
turning once, until crisp and golden.
three Meanwhile, for the salsa, halve the
cucumber, scoop out the seeds and finely
chop. Toss in a bowl with the coriander,
spring onions, lemon or lime juice, sugar and
a little salt and pepper.
four Split the rolls and sandwich with the
burgers and salsa. Serve with salad.

Sun-dried tomato pesto has all the vibrant flavour of the better-known basil version (see page 8), and serves equally as many uses. Try it spread on to pizzas, tossed with pasta or stirred into vegetable soups and stews.

toasted goats' cheese with sun-dried tomato pesto

preparation time **10 mins**
cooking time **5 mins**
total time **15 mins** serves **4**

4 chunky slices of walnut or grainy bread
250 g/8 oz goats' cheese
leafy salad, to serve

SUN-DRIED TOMATO PESTO
125 g/4 oz sun-dried tomatoes in oil, drained
4 tablespoons pine nuts
10 pitted black olives
2 garlic cloves, roughly chopped
5 tablespoons olive oil
25 g/1 oz Parmesan cheese, grated
salt and pepper

one To make the pesto, place the sun-dried tomatoes in a food processor or blender with the pine nuts, olives and garlic. Process until chopped.

two With the motor running, add the oil in a thin, steady stream. Once combined, turn into a bowl and stir in the Parmesan cheese and salt and pepper.

three Toast one side of the bread under a preheated moderate grill. Turn the bread over and top with the goats' cheese. Increase the heat and grill until the cheese is melting and golden. Transfer to serving plates and spoon over the pesto. Serve with a leafy salad.

tortillas with minted chilli and aubergine yogurt

preparation time **10 mins**
cooking time **10 mins**
total time **20 mins** serves **2**

4 tablespoons olive oil
1 medium aubergine, thinly sliced
small handful of mint, chopped
small handful of parsley, chopped
2 tablespoons chopped chives
1 green chilli, deseeded and thinly sliced
200 ml/7 fl oz Greek yogurt
2 tablespoons mayonnaise
2 large tortillas
7 cm/3 inch length of cucumber, thinly sliced
salt and pepper
paprika, to garnish

one Heat the oil in a frying pan. Add the aubergine and fry for about 10 minutes until golden. Drain and set aside to cool.

two Mix the herbs with the chilli, yogurt and mayonnaise in a bowl and season to taste with salt and pepper.

three Arrange the fried aubergine slices over the tortillas and spread with the Greek yogurt mixture. Arrange the cucumber slices on top. Roll up each tortilla, sprinkle with paprika and serve.

pancakes
and pastries

Whether made from batter or vegetables, pancakes can be classic or inventive, taking on a main meal role with an eclectic mix of tempting toppings and fillings to suit your tastes and moods. Extend the variety by using ready-made pastries, such as mouth-wateringly crisp filo and rich, golden puff pastry, for great results in just a few minutes.

filo, pesto and mozzarella parcels

preparation time **10 mins**
cooking time **10 mins**
total time **20 mins** serves **4**

125 g/4 oz filo pastry sheets
50 g/2 oz butter, melted
3 tablespoons Sun-dried Tomato Pesto
  (see page 65)
250 g/8 oz mozzarella cheese, drained
  and sliced
50 g/2 oz Parmesan cheese, grated
salt and pepper
leafy salad, to serve

one Cut the filo pastry into 16 15-cm/6-inch squares. Lay 8 squares on the work surface and brush with a little melted butter. Cover each with a second square.
two Dot the pesto into the centres of the squares and spread slightly. Arrange the mozzarella and Parmesan over the pesto. Season lightly with salt and pepper.
three Bring two opposite sides of the pastry over the filling to enclose completely. Lightly brush with butter, then fold over the two open ends to make parcels. Place on a baking sheet with the ends uppermost.
four Brush with the remaining butter (melt a little more if necessary) and bake in a preheated oven, 200°C (400°F), Gas Mark 6, for about 10 minutes until golden. Serve warm with a leafy salad.

camembert and shallot tarts

preparation time **10 mins**
cooking time **20 mins**
total time **30 mins** serves **4**

50 g/2 oz butter
8 large shallots, each cut into 4 wedges
1 tablespoon chopped lemon thyme
350 g/11½ oz puff pastry
125 g/4 oz Camembert cheese, sliced
salt and pepper

one Lightly grease a baking sheet and sprinkle with water. Melt the butter in a frying pan, add the shallots and gently fry for 5 minutes until softened. Stir in the thyme.
two Roll out the pastry on a lightly floured surface to a 20 cm/8 inch square and cut into 4 squares. Transfer to the prepared baking sheet. Using the tip of a sharp knife, make a shallow cut along each side of the squares, 1 cm/½ inch from the edges, to form a rim.
three Spoon the shallots and thyme into the centres of the pastries. Bake in a preheated oven, 220°C (425°F), Gas Mark 7, for 10 minutes until well risen. Arrange the cheese over the shallots and return to the oven for a further 5 minutes. Serve warm.

courgette pancakes with emmental and peppers

preparation time **10 mins**
cooking time **20 mins**
total time **30 mins** serves **6**

325 g/11 oz courgettes
175 g/6 oz plain flour
3 eggs
75 g/3 oz butter, melted
125 ml/4 fl oz milk
1 tablespoon chopped thyme
6 tablespoons olive oil
300 g/10 oz aubergine, cut into small chunks
2 small red onions, sliced
2 red peppers, cored, deseeded and sliced
400 g/13 oz can chopped tomatoes
2 tablespoons balsamic vinegar
oil, for shallow-frying
300 g/10 oz Emmental cheese, thinly sliced
salt and pepper

These crisp little pancakes, topped with melting cheese and a ratatouille-style topping, make a thoroughly enjoyable starter, or increase the size of the pancakes and serve with a salad for a main course.

one Grate the courgettes. In a large bowl, beat together the flour, eggs, butter, milk and thyme to make a smooth batter. Stir in the grated courgettes and season with salt and pepper.

two Heat the olive oil in a large, heavy-based saucepan or sauté pan. Add the aubergine and onions and fry for about 5 minutes until turning golden. Add the peppers and continue frying quickly for about 3 minutes until the vegetables are lightly browned. Add the tomatoes, vinegar and salt and pepper. Reduce the heat and simmer gently, uncovered, for 10 minutes while preparing the pancakes.

three Heat a little oil in a large frying pan. Add a tablespoonful of the pancake mixture to one side of the pan and spread to about 10 cm/4 inches. Add as many more spoonfuls of the batter as the pan will contain and fry for about 2 minutes until golden on the underside. Turn the pancakes and cook for a further 2 minutes. Drain on kitchen paper and transfer to a grill pan. Cook the remainder of the pancakes (the mixture should make 12 in total).

four Arrange the cheese slices over the pancakes and grill under a preheated hot grill until the cheese is melting. Arrange 2 pancakes on each serving plate, overlapping them slightly. Pile the pepper sauce on top and serve warm.

cherry tomato tarts with pesto crème fraîche

preparation time **10 mins**
cooking time **18 mins**
total time **28 mins** serves **4**

2 tablespoons extra virgin olive oil
1 onion, finely chopped
375 g/12 oz cherry tomatoes
2 garlic cloves, crushed
3 tablespoons sun-dried tomato paste
325 g/11 oz puff pastry
beaten egg, to glaze
150 g/5 oz crème fraîche
2 tablespoons Pesto (see page 8)
salt and pepper
basil leaves, to garnish

one Lightly grease a large baking sheet and sprinkle with water. Heat the oil in a frying pan, add the onion and fry for about 3 minutes until softened. Halve about 150 g/5 oz of the tomatoes. Remove the pan from the heat, add the garlic and sun-dried tomato paste, then stir in all the tomatoes, turning until they are lightly coated in the sauce.

two Roll out the pastry on a lightly floured surface and cut out four 12 cm/5 inch rounds using a cutter or small bowl as a guide. Transfer to the prepared baking sheet and make a shallow cut 1 cm/½ inch from the edge of each round using the tip of a sharp knife, to form a rim. Brush the rims with beaten egg. Pile the tomato mixture on to the centres of the pastries, making sure the mixture stays within the rims.

three Bake the tartlets in a preheated oven, 220°C (425°F), Gas Mark 7, for about 15 minutes until the pastry is risen and golden.

four Meanwhile, lightly mix together the crème fraîche, pesto and salt and pepper in a bowl so that the crème fraîche is streaked with the pesto.

five When cooked, transfer the tartlets to serving plates and spoon over the crème fraîche and pesto mixture. Serve scattered with basil leaves.

minted pea cake with mozzarella, tomato and basil

preparation time **10 mins**
cooking time **16 mins**
total time **26 mins** serves **4**

500 g/1 lb potatoes
250 g/8 oz peas
3 tablespoons chopped mint
1 egg, lightly beaten
300 g/10 oz mozzarella cheese, sliced
6 plum tomatoes, sliced
6 tablespoons extra virgin olive oil
1 tablespoon balsamic vinegar
small handful of basil leaves, shredded
50 g/2 oz butter
salt and pepper

one Cut the potatoes into chunks and cook in lightly salted boiling water for about 8 minutes until softened but still retaining their firm texture.

two Meanwhile, cook the peas in a separate pan of lightly salted boiling water for 2 minutes. Drain the peas and place in a bowl, then mash with a fork until broken up. Coarsely grate the potatoes and add to the bowl with the mint, beaten egg and salt and pepper. Mix together until evenly combined.

three Arrange alternate overlapping slices of the cheese and tomatoes in a shallow flameproof dish and season lightly with salt and pepper. Mix 5 tablespoons of the olive oil with the vinegar and basil for the dressing.

four Melt the butter with the remaining oil in a heavy-based frying pan. Add the potato and pea mixture and pack down gently in an even layer. Fry over a moderate heat for about 5 minutes until the underside looks crisp and golden when the edge is lifted with a palette knife.

five To turn the pancake, invert it on to a baking sheet or flat plate, then slide it back into the pan and fry for a further 3 minutes. While it is cooking, grill the cheese and tomatoes under a preheated hot grill until the cheese starts to melt.

six Cut the pancake into wedges and transfer to serving plates. Pile the cheese and tomatoes on top and spoon over the dressing.

tofu, cinnamon and honey parcels

preparation time **15 mins**
cooking time **15 mins**
total time **30 mins** serves **4**

50 g/2 oz butter
2 onions, chopped
50 g/2 oz flaked almonds, lightly crushed
1 tablespoon clear honey
1 teaspoon ground cinnamon
200 g/7 oz tofu, drained and diced
150 g/5 oz filo pastry
salt and pepper

one Melt half of the butter in a frying pan,
add the onions and fry for 3 minutes until
softened. Stir in the almonds and fry for
2 minutes until turning golden. Stir in the
honey, cinnamon and tofu, and season to
taste with salt and pepper.
two Melt the remaining butter in a small
saucepan. Cut out 16 18-cm/7-inch squares
from the filo pastry. Lay 8 squares on a work
surface and brush with a little melted butter.
Cover each with a second square placed at
an angle to create a star shape. Pile the tofu
mixture on to the centres of the squares.
three Brush the edges of the pastry with
a little butter. Bring the edges up over the
filling and pinch together to make bundles.
Repeat with the remaining pastries.
Transfer to a baking sheet and brush with
the remaining butter.
four Bake in a preheated oven, 200°C
(400°F), Gas Mark 6, for about 10 minutes
until the pastry is golden. Serve warm.

These tasty chickpea cakes, traditionally
rolled into little balls and deep fried,
make a great veggie supper served simply
with a fresh, Greek-style salad.

falafel cakes

preparation time **10 mins**
cooking time **10 mins**
total time **20 mins** serves **4**

400 g/13 oz can chickpeas, rinsed
   and drained
1 onion, roughly chopped
3 garlic cloves, roughly chopped
2 teaspoons cumin seeds
1 teaspoon mild chilli powder
2 tablespoons chopped mint
3 tablespoons chopped coriander
50 g/2 oz breadcrumbs
oil, for shallow-frying
salt and pepper

one Place the chickpeas in a food processor
or blender with the onion, garlic, spices,
herbs, breadcrumbs and a little salt and
pepper. Blend briefly to make a chunky paste.
two Take dessertspoonfuls of the mixture
and flatten into cakes. Heat a 1 cm/$\frac{1}{2}$ inch
depth of oil in a frying pan and fry half the
falafel for about 3 minutes, turning once until
crisp and golden. Drain on kitchen paper and
keep warm while cooking the remainder.

lemon grass and tofu nuggets with chilli sauce

preparation time **10 mins**
cooking time **10 mins**
total time **20 mins** serves **4**

1 bunch of spring onions
5 cm/2 inch piece of fresh root ginger, peeled
   and chopped
2 lemon grass stalks, roughly chopped
small handful of coriander
3 garlic cloves, roughly chopped
1 tablespoon caster sugar
1 tablespoon light soy sauce
300 g/10 oz tofu, drained
75 g/3 oz breadcrumbs
1 egg
oil, for shallow-frying
salt and pepper

DIPPING SAUCE
1 tablespoon clear honey
2 tablespoons soy sauce
1 red chilli, deseeded and sliced
2 tablespoons orange juice

one Thinly slice 1 spring onion and set aside. Roughly chop the remainder and place in a food processor with the ginger, lemon grass, coriander and garlic. Process lightly until mixed together and chopped but still chunky. Add the sugar, soy sauce, tofu, breadcrumbs, egg and salt and pepper and process until just combined.

two Take dessertspoonfuls of the mixture and pat into flat cakes using lightly floured hands.

three Mix together the ingredients for the dipping sauce, adding the reserved sliced spring onion, in a small serving bowl.

four Heat the oil in a large nonstick frying pan. Add half the tofu cakes and fry gently for 1–2 minutes on each side until golden. Drain on kitchen paper and keep warm while frying the remainder. Serve with the dipping sauce.

vegetable rice pancakes with sesame and ginger sauce

preparation time **15 mins**
cooking time **5 mins**
total time **20 mins** serves **4**

SAUCE
1 garlic clove, roughly chopped
5 cm/2 inch piece fresh root ginger, peeled
   and roughly chopped
3 tablespoons light muscovado sugar
4 teaspoons soy sauce
5 teaspoons wine or rice vinegar
2 tablespoons tomato purée
2 tablespoons sesame seeds, plus extra
   to garnish

PANCAKES
8 rice pancakes
2 medium carrots
100 g/3½ oz bean sprouts or mixed
   sprouting beans
small handful of mint, roughly chopped
1 celery stick, thinly sliced
4 spring onions, thinly sliced diagonally
1 tablespoon soy sauce

one Place all the ingredients for the sauce, except the sesame seeds, in a food processor (use the small bowl of a food processor if you have one) or blender and process to a thin paste. Alternatively, crush the garlic, grate the ginger and whisk with the remaining ingredients. Stir in the sesame seeds and transfer to a serving bowl.

two Soften the rice pancakes according to the packet instructions. Cut the carrots into fine shreds and mix with the bean sprouts or sprouting beans, mint, celery, spring onions and soy sauce.

three Divide the vegetable mixture among the 8 pancakes and spoon into the middle of each. Fold in the bottom edge of each pancake to the middle, then roll up from one side to the other to form a pocket.

four Steam the pancakes in a vegetable steamer or bamboo steamer for about 5 minutes until they are heated through. Alternatively, place on a wire rack set over a roasting tin of boiling water and cover with foil. Serve immediately with the sauce, garnished with sesame seeds.

Paper-thin rice pancakes make interesting wraps for a feast of tempting fillings — here, a light vegetable version. Served with a highly flavoured sauce, they make an intriguing starter. Allow 2 rice pancakes per portion, but if there is a lot to follow, one is probably enough.

couscous, polenta and grains

Couscous, polenta, bulgar wheat and millet take their place among the seemingly ever-expanding range of cereal-based products that is now widely available. Each adds its own individual flavour and texture to vegetarian dishes, whether used as an integral ingredient or as a simple accompaniment.

couscous fritters with beetroot and crème fraîche

preparation time **15 mins**
cooking time **5 mins**
total time **20 mins** serves **4**

150 g/5 oz couscous
100 ml/3½ fl oz hot Vegetable Stock
  (see page 9)
4 spring onions, finely chopped
2 garlic cloves, chopped
3 tablespoons chopped parsley
75 g/3 oz pine nuts, roughly chopped
50 g/2 oz ground almonds
finely grated rind of 1 lemon
1 egg
oil, for frying
4 small cooked beetroots, cut into wedges
salt and pepper
flat leaf parsley, to garnish
crème fraîche, to serve

DRESSING
4 tablespoons extra virgin olive oil
1 teaspoon Tabasco sauce
1 tablespoon lemon juice

one Place two-thirds of the couscous in a bowl, add the vegetable stock and leave to stand for 5 minutes. Meanwhile, mix together the ingredients for the dressing in a small bowl.

two When the couscous has absorbed all the stock, fluff up with a fork and stir in the spring onions, garlic, parsley, pine nuts, almonds, lemon rind and egg. Season with salt and pepper and mix until the ingredients bind together.

three Take heaped teaspoonfuls of the mixture and shape into balls. Roll them in the remaining couscous, spread on a plate. Wet your hands before rolling the balls if the mixture starts to stick.

four Heat a 2.5 cm/1 inch depth of oil in a sauté pan or heavy-based saucepan. Add the couscous balls to the oil, half at a time, and fry for about 2 minutes until golden. Drain the first batch on kitchen paper while cooking the remainder.

five Arrange the beetroot wedges on serving plates and pile the fritters beside them. Top with a spoonful of crème fraîche, garnish with parsley and serve with the dressing spooned over the top.

spiced vegetable couscous

preparation time **5 mins**
cooking time **25 mins**
total time **30 mins** serves **4**

250 g/8 oz couscous
4 tablespoons olive oil
1 large onion, chopped
3 garlic cloves, crushed
5 cm/2 inch piece of fresh root ginger, peeled
   and grated
½ teaspoon dried chilli flakes
2 teaspoons each of paprika and
   ground cumin
1 teaspoon ground turmeric
1 cinnamon stick, halved
1 medium sweet potato, diced
425 g/14 oz can chickpeas, rinsed
450 ml/¾ pint Vegetable Stock (see page 9)
75 g/3 oz raisins or sultanas
salt and pepper
coriander leaves, to garnish

one Place the couscous in a shallow
ovenproof dish, pour over 300 ml/½ pint
boiling water and cover. Place in a preheated
oven, 150°C (300°F), Gas Mark 2, while
preparing the vegetables.
two Heat the oil in a large saucepan. Add
the onion, garlic, ginger and spices and fry
gently, stirring, for 5 minutes until golden.
three Add the sweet potato, chickpeas,
stock and dried fruit. Season with salt and
pepper and bring to the boil. Reduce the
heat, cover and simmer for 20 minutes until
the potatoes are tender.
four Fluff up the couscous with a fork and
spoon on to serving plates. Top with the
vegetables and sauce, and serve scattered
with coriander leaves.

If you want to add extra flavour to
the polenta, stir in some fresh chopped
herbs, grated Parmesan or a generous
pat of butter.

soft polenta with gruyère and tomato sauce

preparation time **10 mins**
cooking time **20 mins**
total time **30 mins** serves **4**

250 g/8 oz instant polenta
3 garlic cloves, chopped
4 tablespoons olive oil
1 large onion, chopped
400 g/13 oz can chopped tomatoes
3 tablespoons sun-dried tomato paste
2 teaspoons light muscovado sugar
75 g/3 oz Gruyère or Cheddar cheese, grated
salt and pepper

one Bring 1 litre/1¾ pints water to the boil in
a large saucepan with 1 teaspoon salt. Add
the polenta in a steady stream, then the
garlic and cook, stirring, for 5 minutes until
the polenta is very thick and pulpy. Turn into
a lightly greased shallow ovenproof dish.
two Heat the oil in a saucepan. Add the
onion and fry for 5 minutes. Add the
tomatoes, sun-dried tomato paste and sugar
to the onion and season to taste with salt and
pepper. Spoon the mixture over the polenta.
three Scatter with the grated cheese and
bake in a preheated oven, 200°C (400°F),
Gas Mark 6, for 10 minutes until golden.

green couscous with spiced fruit sauce

preparation time **10 mins**
cooking time **15 mins**
total time **25 mins** serves **4**

250 g/8 oz couscous
500 ml/17 fl oz hot Vegetable Stock
   (see page 9)
75 g/3 oz unsalted, shelled pistachio
   nuts, roughly chopped
2 spring onions, chopped
small handful of parsley, chopped
425 g/14 oz can flageolet beans, rinsed
   and drained
½ teaspoon saffron threads
1 tablespoon cardamom pods
2 teaspoons coriander seeds
½ teaspoon chilli powder
4 tablespoons flaked almonds
75 g/3 oz ready-to-eat dried apricots
salt and pepper

To reveal their stunning emerald green colour, pistachio nuts are best skinned by immersing them in boiling water for one minute, then rubbing off the skins between sheets of kitchen paper. Only do this if you have time since it is very labour-intensive!

one Place the couscous in a bowl. Add 300 ml/½ pint of the hot stock. Leave to stand for 5 minutes until the stock is absorbed, then stir in the pistachio nuts, spring onions, parsley and beans, season to taste with salt and pepper. Cover the bowl and place in a preheated oven, 150°C (300°F), Gas Mark 2, for 15 minutes.

two Meanwhile, place the saffron in a small cup with 1 tablespoon boiling water and leave for 3 minutes. Crush the cardamom pods using a pestle and mortar, or place the pods in a small bowl and crush with the end of a rolling pin. Pick out and discard the pods, then lightly crush the seeds.

three Transfer to a food processor or blender with the coriander seeds, chilli powder, almonds and apricots. Process until finely chopped. Add the saffron and soaking liquid, the remaining stock and salt and pepper and blend until pulpy. Transfer to a saucepan and heat through for 1 minute. Serve with the couscous.

An abundance of herbs gives this salad its wonderful flavour. If prunes are not your favourite dried fruit, substitute just about any other — apricots, plump sultanas or raisins. Figs and dates are also good in this recipe.

tabbouleh with fruit and nuts

preparation time **10 mins**, plus soaking
total time **25 mins** serves **4**

150 g/5 oz bulgar wheat
75 g/3 oz unsalted, shelled pistachio nuts
1 small red onion, finely chopped
3 garlic cloves, crushed
25 g/1 oz flat leaf parsley, chopped
15 g/½ oz mint, chopped
finely grated rind and juice of 1 lemon
   or lime
150 g/5 oz ready-to-eat prunes, sliced
4 tablespoons olive oil
salt and pepper

one Place the bulgar wheat in a bowl, cover with plenty of boiling water and leave to soak for 15 minutes.

two Meanwhile, place the pistachio nuts in a separate bowl and cover with boiling water. Leave to stand for 1 minute, then drain. Rub the nuts between several thicknesses of kitchen paper to remove most of the skins, then peel away any remaining skins with the fingers.

three Mix the nuts with the onion, garlic, parsley, mint, lemon or lime rind and juice and prunes in a large bowl.

four Drain the bulgar wheat thoroughly in a sieve, pressing out as much moisture as possible with the back of a spoon. Add to the other ingredients with the oil and toss together. Season to taste with salt and pepper and chill until ready to serve.

mushroom, couscous and herb sausages

preparation time **15 mins**
cooking time **10 mins**
total time **25 mins** serves **4**

75 g/3 oz couscous
3 tablespoons olive oil
1 onion, chopped
250 g/8 oz chestnut mushrooms,
   roughly chopped
1 red chilli, deseeded and finely sliced
3 garlic cloves, roughly chopped
small handful of mixed herbs, such as thyme,
   rosemary, parsley
200 g/7 oz whole cooked chestnuts
75 g/3 oz breadcrumbs
1 egg yolk
oil, for shallow-frying
salt and pepper

one Place the couscous in a bowl, add 75 ml/3 fl oz boiling water and leave to stand for 5 minutes.

two Meanwhile, heat the olive oil in a frying pan, add the onion, mushrooms and chilli and fry quickly for about 5 minutes until the mushrooms are golden and the moisture has evaporated.

three Transfer to a food processor or blender with the garlic, herbs and chestnuts and process until finely chopped. Turn into a bowl and add the soaked couscous, breadcrumbs, egg yolk and salt and pepper.

four Using lightly floured hands, shape the mixture into 12 sausage shapes. Heat the oil for shallow-frying and fry the sausages for about 5 minutes, turning frequently.

Millet is a small, golden grain that looks a little like couscous, and makes a perfect alternative to rice. Add some drained, canned lentils and a spoonful of harissa paste to turn this dish into a main course.

spiced millet

preparation time **5 mins**
cooking time **25 mins**
total time **30 mins** serves **4**

50 g/2 oz butter
1 onion, chopped
2 garlic cloves, crushed
1 tablespoon cardamom pods, lightly crushed
2 teaspoons whole cloves
1 cinnamon stick, halved
200 g/7 oz millet
600 ml/1 pint Vegetable Stock
  (see page 9)
4 tablespoons chopped parsley
salt and pepper

one Melt the butter in a heavy-based saucepan. Add the onion and fry gently for 3 minutes. Add the garlic, cardamom pods, cloves, cinnamon and millet. Season to taste with salt and pepper and fry for 2 minutes.
two Add the stock and the parsley and bring to the boil. Reduce the heat and simmer gently, uncovered, for about 20 minutes until the millet is tender and the stock absorbed. Lightly fork up the millet a couple of times during cooking to keep the grains light and separate. Serve hot.

polenta chips with saffron mushrooms

preparation time **10 mins**
cooking time **20 mins**
total time **30 mins** serves **4**

1 teaspoon saffron threads
500 g/1 lb ready-cooked polenta
1 tablespoon plain flour
2 teaspoons chilli powder
oil, for shallow-frying
25 g/1 oz butter
1 onion, chopped
2 garlic cloves, crushed
400 g/13 oz mixed wild and cultivated
  mushrooms, halved if large
250 g/8 oz mascarpone cheese
2 tablespoons chopped tarragon
finely grated rind and juice of ½ lemon
salt and pepper

one Place the saffron in a bowl with 1 tablespoon boiling water and leave to stand.
two Cut the polenta into 1 cm/½ inch slices, then cut the slices into 1 cm/½ inch chips. Mix together the flour, chilli powder and salt and pepper and use to coat the polenta.
three Heat a 1 cm/½ inch depth of oil in a frying pan and fry the chips, half at a time, for about 10 minutes until golden. Once cooked, drain on kitchen paper and keep warm.
four Meanwhile, melt the butter in a separate frying pan, add the onion and garlic and fry for 5 minutes. Stir in the mushrooms and fry for 2 minutes. Add the mascarpone, tarragon, lemon rind and juice, saffron and soaking liquid, and season with salt and pepper. Stir until the mascarpone has melted to make a sauce. Serve with the polenta chips.

Unless you have the time to cook and set homemade polenta,
use a pack of ready-cooked polenta to make these chips.
Tossed in chilli powder and shallow-fried, they make a
welcome change to the more traditional potato chips.

salads and side salads

Creativity is the key when it comes to salads, composing with several carefully selected complementary ingredients to create a feast of colour, flavour and texture. Some of the salads presented are sufficiently sustaining to serve as main courses, while others make attractive starters or imaginative side dishes.

ribboned carrot salad

preparation time **10 mins**, plus soaking
total time **25–30 mins** serves **4**

4 medium carrots
2 celery sticks
1 bunch of spring onions
4 tablespoons light olive oil
2 tablespoons lime juice
2 teaspoons caster sugar
¼ teaspoon crushed dried chillies
2 tablespoons chopped mint
50 g/2 oz salted peanuts
salt and pepper

one Half fill a medium bowl with very cold
water, adding a few ice cubes if necessary.
two Scrub the carrots and pare off as many
long ribbons as you can from each. Place
the ribbons in the water. Cut the celery into
5 cm/2 inch lengths. Cut each length into
very thin slices. Cut the spring onions into
5 cm/2 inch lengths and shred lengthways.
Add the celery and spring onions to the
water and leave for 15–20 minutes until the
vegetables curl up.
three Mix together the oil, lime juice, sugar,
chillies and mint in a small bowl and season
to taste with salt and pepper.
four Thoroughly drain the vegetables and
toss in a salad bowl with the dressing,
peanuts and salt and pepper. Serve the
salad immediately.

sweet potato, rocket and haloumi salad

preparation time **10 mins**
cooking time **15 mins**
total time **25 mins** serves **4**

500 g/1 lb sweet potatoes, sliced
3 tablespoons olive oil
250 g/8 oz haloumi cheese, patted
    dry on kitchen paper
75 g/3 oz rocket

DRESSING
5 tablespoons olive oil
3 tablespoons clear honey
2 tablespoons lemon or lime juice
1½ teaspoons black onion seeds
1 red chilli, deseeded and finely sliced
2 teaspoons chopped lemon thyme
salt and pepper

one Mix together all the ingredients for
the dressing in a small bowl.
two Cook the sweet potatoes in lightly
salted boiling water for 2 minutes. Drain
well. Heat the oil in a large frying pan, add
the sweet potatoes and fry for about
10 minutes, turning once, until golden.
three Meanwhile, thinly slice the cheese
and place on a lightly oiled foil-lined grill
rack. Cook under a preheated moderate
grill for about 3 minutes until golden.
four Pile the sweet potatoes, cheese and
rocket on to serving plates and spoon over
the dressing.

This combination of firm, salty cheese, sweet potato and a honeyed, spiced citrus dressing is absolutely delicious. This quantity serves 4 as a light lunch or supper dish, or 6 as a starter.

grilled baby aubergine and tomato salad

preparation time **10 mins**
cooking time **10 mins**
total time **20 mins** serves **4**

275 g/9 oz baby aubergines
4 tablespoons olive oil
1 tablespoon lemon juice
2 tablespoons roughly chopped chervil
  or parsley
250 g/8 oz cherry tomatoes, halved
1 teaspoon caster sugar
2 garlic cloves, crushed
200 g/7 oz ricotta cheese
50 g/2 oz rocket
4 teaspoons balsamic vinegar
salt and pepper

Serve this colourful salad either as a starter for 4 or a more substantial supper for 2. Although very appealing, baby aubergines are not widely available, so substitute a large aubergine, thickly sliced, if you cannot find any.

one Halve the aubergines and cut criss-cross lines over the cut surfaces for decoration. Place, cut sides up, on a foil-lined grill rack and drizzle with 1 tablespoon of the oil, the lemon juice and salt and pepper. Grill under a preheated hot grill for 8–10 minutes, turning once, until the slices are tender and golden, then sprinkle them with the chervil or parsley.

two Meanwhile, place the tomatoes in a frying pan with another tablespoon of the oil and sprinkle with the sugar, garlic and salt and pepper. Fry quickly for 1–2 minutes until softened but not mushy.

three Arrange the aubergines on warmed serving plates, pile the ricotta, then the tomatoes and finally the rocket on top. Add the balsamic vinegar, the remaining oil, salt and pepper and any juices on the foil to the frying pan and heat through for 30 seconds. Pour over the salad before serving.

thai-dressed tofu rolls

preparation time **10 mins**
total time **10 mins** serves **4**

1 small iceburg lettuce
275 g/9 oz tofu, diced
100 g/3½ oz mangetout, shredded lengthways
2 tablespoons sesame oil
2 tablespoons light soy sauce
2 tablespoons lime juice
1 tablespoon muscovado sugar
1 Thai chilli, deseeded and sliced
1 garlic clove, crushed
pepper

one Remove 8 leaves from the lettuce. Fill a large heatproof bowl with boiling water. Add the separated leaves and leave for 10 seconds. Rinse in cold water and drain thoroughly.
two Finely shred the remaining lettuce and toss in a bowl with the tofu and mangetout.
three Mix together the sesame oil, soy sauce, lime juice, sugar, chilli, garlic and pepper and add to the tofu mixture. Toss together gently, using 2 spoons.
four Spoon a little mixture on to the centre of each blanched lettuce leaf, then roll up. Chill until ready to serve.

beetroot salad with coriander and tomato salsa

preparation time **10 mins**
total time **10 mins** serves **4**

8 medium cooked beetroots, sliced
2 tablespoons red wine vinegar
1 teaspoon caster sugar
2 tablespoons light olive oil
salt and pepper
crème fraîche, to serve
coriander sprigs, to garnish

SALSA
1 red onion, finely chopped
425 g/14 oz small vine-ripened tomatoes, deseeded and chopped
2 garlic cloves, crushed
15 g/½ oz coriander, chopped

one Toss the beetroot in a bowl with the vinegar, sugar, oil and salt and pepper.
two Mix together the ingredients for the salsa in a separate bowl. Season lightly with salt and pepper.
three Arrange about two-thirds of the beetroot slices on 4 serving plates. Pile the salsa on to the beetroot, then add the remaining beetroot slices. Top with spoonfuls of crème fraîche and spoon over any dressing left in the beetroot bowl. Serve garnished with coriander sprigs.

spiced orange
and avocado salad

preparation time **10 mins**
total time **10 mins** serves **4**

4 large juicy oranges
2 small ripe avocados, stoned and peeled
2 teaspoons cardamom pods
3 tablespoons light olive oil
1 tablespoon clear honey
good pinch of ground allspice
2 teaspoons lemon juice
salt and pepper
watercress sprigs, to garnish

one Cut the skin and the white membrane
off the oranges. Working over a bowl to
catch the juice, cut between the
membranes to remove the segments.
two Slice the avocados and toss gently
with the orange segments. Pile on to
serving plates.
three Reserve a few whole cardamom pods
for decoration. Crush the remaining pods
using a pestle and mortar to extract the
seeds, or place in a small bowl and crush
with the end of a rolling pin. Pick out and
discard the pods. Mix the seeds with the oil,
honey, allspice, lemon juice, salt and pepper
and reserved orange juice.
four Garnish the salads with the watercress
sprigs and serve with the dressing spooned
over the top.

This refreshing, summery side salad
can easily be transformed into a main
course with the addition of diced
smoked tofu or goats' cheese. Serve
with a grainy, malty bread.

herb salad with stem
ginger and grapes

preparation time **5 mins**
total time **5 mins** serves **4**

1 small head of fennel, finely chopped
250 g/8 oz seedless white grapes, halved
2 pieces of bottled stem ginger, finely chopped
2 tablespoons syrup from the ginger jar
4 tablespoons grape or apple juice
2 tablespoons olive oil
150 g/5 oz mixed herb or leaf salad
50 g/2 oz unsalted cashews or walnuts
   (optional)
salt and pepper

one In a medium bowl, mix together the
fennel, grapes, ginger and ginger syrup, fruit
juice and oil, and season to taste with salt
and pepper.
two Place the salad leaves in a serving
bowl and add the nuts, if using. Add the
other ingredients and toss lightly together
before serving.

potato and french bean salad

preparation time **10 mins**
cooking time **15 mins**
total time **25 mins** serves **4**

875 g/1¾ lb new potatoes, scrubbed
150 g/5 oz French beans, halved
6 tablespoons extra virgin olive oil
4 teaspoons lemon juice
2 teaspoons pink peppercorns
1 teaspoon caster sugar
4 tablespoons chopped chives
4 eggs
salt and pepper
watercress or sorrel, to serve

one Cook the potatoes in plenty of lightly salted boiling water for about 15 minutes or until just tender.
two Meanwhile, cook the French beans in a separate pan of boiling water for 2–3 minutes until just tender. Drain and refresh under cold water.
three Mix together the oil, lemon juice, peppercorns, sugar, chives and salt and pepper in a bowl.
four Lower the eggs into a small saucepan of boiling water and cook for 4 minutes. (Cook the eggs for an extra 3 minutes if you prefer them hard-boiled.) Drain.
five Drain the potatoes, then immerse in a bowl of water to cool. Drain. Shell and quarter the eggs.
six Toss the potatoes, French beans and eggs in the dressing. Pile on to a bed of watercress or sorrel on individual serving plates.

panzanella

preparation time **15 mins**
cooking time **10 mins**
total time **25 mins** serves **4**

3 red peppers, cored, deseeded and quartered
375 g/12 oz ripe plum tomatoes, skinned
6 tablespoons extra virgin olive oil
3 tablespoons wine vinegar
2 garlic cloves, crushed
125 g/4 oz stale ciabatta bread
50 g/2 oz pitted black olives
small handful of basil leaves, shredded
salt and pepper

one Place the peppers, skin side up, on a foil-lined grill rack and grill under a preheated moderate grill for 10 minutes or until the skins are blackened.
two Meanwhile, quarter the tomatoes and scoop out the pulp, placing it in a sieve over a bowl to catch the juices. Set the tomato quarters aside. Press the pulp with the back of a spoon to extract as much juice as possible.
three Beat the oil, vinegar, garlic and salt and pepper into the tomato juice.
four When cool enough to handle, peel the skins from the peppers and discard. Roughly slice the peppers and place in a bowl with the tomato quarters. Break the bread into small chunks and add to the bowl with the olives and basil.
five Add the dressing and toss the ingredients together before serving.

In this classic Italian salad, pieces of ciabatta are tossed with the other ingredients, absorbing the wonderful flavour of the garlicky tomato dressing. It is best to use slightly stale ciabatta which will not fall apart. Alternatively, use lightly toasted fresh bread. This quantity serves 4 as a starter or 2 as a main course.

vegetable dishes

Vegetarian cooking thrives on the amazing array of exotic, seasonal and everyday vegetables that we can now readily buy, and the many different ways in which they can be cooked. Here, fresh herbs, fragrant spices and other subtle seasonings are used to bring out the essential flavours of the ingredients to create delicious main meals, snacks and accompaniments.

devilled mushrooms on brioche

preparation time **5 mins**
cooking time **7 mins**
total time **12 mins** serves **2**

4 teaspoons mango chutney
1.5 cm/¾ inch piece of fresh root ginger,
   peeled and grated
2 tablespoons Worcestershire sauce
1 tablespoon coarse-grain mustard
2 teaspoons paprika
5 tablespoons fresh orange juice
2 brioche buns or 2 large slices of brioche
25 g/1 oz butter
1 tablespoon oil
3 shallots, thinly sliced
250 g/8 oz chestnut mushrooms, halved
2 tablespoons soured cream

one Cut up any large pieces of mango
and mix the chutney with the ginger,
Worcestershire sauce, mustard, paprika
and orange juice.
two Thickly slice the buns, if using, and
toast the brioche. Keep warm.
three Melt the butter in a frying pan with
the oil. Add the shallots and fry gently for
3 minutes until softened. Add the
mushrooms and fry quickly for about
3 minutes, stirring, until golden.
four Add the chutney mixture to the pan
and heat through for 1 minute, then stir in
the cream. Spoon over the toasted brioche
and serve hot.

celeriac and potato remoulade with asparagus

preparation time **10 mins**
cooking time **7 mins**
total time **17 mins** serves **4**

500 g/1 lb celeriac, peeled
375 g/12 oz potatoes, peeled
1 tablespoon extra virgin olive oil,
   plus extra for drizzling (optional)
500 g/1 lb asparagus, trimmed

SAUCE
150 ml/¼ pint mayonnaise
150 ml/¼ pint Greek yogurt
1 teaspoon Dijon mustard
6 cocktail gherkins, finely chopped
2 tablespoons capers, chopped
2 tablespoons chopped tarragon
salt and pepper

one Cut the celeriac and potato into
matchstick-sized pieces, but keep the two
vegetables separate. Cook the celeriac in
lightly salted boiling water for 2 minutes
until softened. Add the potatoes and cook
for a further 2 minutes until just tender.
Drain the vegetables and refresh under
running water.
two Meanwhile, mix together the
ingredients for the sauce and set aside.
three Heat the oil in a frying pan or griddle
pan. Add the asparagus and fry for 2–3
minutes until just beginning to colour.
four Mix the celeriac and potato with the
sauce and spoon on to 4 serving plates.
Top with the asparagus spears.
five Serve immediately, drizzled with a little
extra olive oil, if liked.

To make this summery lunch or supper dish
more substantial, lightly poach some eggs
and arrange them over the asparagus.

wilted spinach with pine nuts and raisins

preparation time **5 mins**
cooking time **2 mins**
total time **7 mins** serves **4**

50 g/2 oz plump raisins
3 tablespoons olive oil
40 g/1½ oz pine nuts
2 garlic cloves, crushed
625 g/1¼ lb baby spinach
finely grated rind of 1 lemon
salt and pepper

one Place the raisins in a small bowl, cover with boiling water and leave for 5 minutes.
two Meanwhile, heat the oil in a large frying pan or sauté pan and fry the pine nuts until pale golden. Stir in the garlic.
three Thoroughly drain the raisins and add to the pan with the spinach. Cook for about 1 minute, turning the ingredients together until the spinach has just wilted. Add the lemon rind, season to taste with salt and pepper and serve immediately.

This refreshing combination of flavours makes a good accompaniment to pizza, bean or pasta dishes, or serve as a light tapas on its own to excite the appetite.

deep-fried courgettes with minted yogurt

preparation time **10 mins**
cooking time **10 mins**
total time **20 mins** serves **4**

3 medium courgettes
1 small onion, very thinly sliced
1 egg
½ teaspoon medium curry paste
100 g/3½ fl oz plain flour
oil, for deep-frying

MINTED YOGURT
7 tablespoons Greek yogurt
2 tablespoons chopped mint

one Coarsely grate the courgettes and mix in a bowl with the onion.
two In a separate bowl, beat the egg with the curry paste and 100 ml/3½ fl oz cold water. Whisk in the flour. Add the courgettes and onions and mix until evenly combined.
three Mix the yogurt with the mint in a small serving dish.
four Heat a 5 cm/2 inch depth of oil in a deep-fat fryer or large, heavy-based saucepan until a drop of the batter sizzles and rises to the surface. Add heaped dessertspoonfuls of the batter to the pan and fry for about 3 minutes until crisp and golden. Drain on kitchen paper and keep warm while cooking the remainder. You will probably need to fry the batter in 3 batches. Serve with the minted yogurt.

mushroom toad-in-the-hole with beer and onion gravy

preparation time **5 mins**
cooking time **25 mins**
total time **30 mins** serves **4**

4 large Portobello mushrooms,
    or 400 g/13 oz smaller open mushrooms
25 g/1 oz butter
5 tablespoons olive oil
3 garlic cloves, sliced
2 tablespoons chopped rosemary
    or thyme
125 g/4 oz plain flour
2 eggs
2 tablespoons hot horseradish sauce
400 ml/14 fl oz milk
2 onions, sliced
2 teaspoons caster sugar
275 ml/9 fl oz stout
150 ml/¼ pint Vegetable Stock
    (see page 9)
salt and pepper

one Place the mushrooms, stalk sides up, in a large shallow ovenproof dish. Melt the butter with 4 tablespoons of the oil in a frying pan. Add the garlic and herbs, season to taste with salt and pepper and stir for 30 seconds. Pour the mixture over the mushrooms. Bake in a preheated oven, 230°C (450°F), Gas Mark 8, for 2 minutes.
two Meanwhile, blend the flour, eggs, horseradish, milk and a little salt in a food processor or blender until smooth. Alternatively, place the flour in a bowl and gradually whisk in the eggs, horseradish, milk and a little salt.
three Pour the batter over the mushrooms and bake for 20–25 minutes until the batter is well risen and golden.
four Meanwhile, heat the remaining oil in a frying pan. Add the onions and sugar and fry for about 5 minutes until deep golden. Add the beer and stock and season to taste with salt and pepper. Cook, stirring frequently, for 5 minutes. Serve poured over the mushroom batter.

baby squash with red bean sauce

preparation time **10 mins**
cooking time **15 mins**
total time **25 mins** serves **4**

600 ml/1 pint Vegetable Stock
  (see page 9)
1 kg/2 lb mixed baby squash,
  such as gem, butternut or acorn
125 g/4 oz baby spinach

SAUCE
4 tablespoons olive oil
4 garlic cloves, thinly sliced
1 red pepper, cored, deseeded and
  finely chopped
2 tomatoes, chopped
425 g/14 oz can red kidney beans, rinsed
  and drained
1–2 tablespoons hot chilli sauce
small handful of coriander, chopped
salt

TO SERVE
steamed white rice
soured cream (optional)
avocado and lime salad (optional)

one Bring the stock to the boil in a large saucepan. Quarter and deseed the squash. Add to the pan, reduce the heat and cover. Simmer gently for about 15 minutes or until the squash are just tender.

two Meanwhile, to make the sauce, heat the oil in a frying pan, add the garlic and pepper and fry for 5 minutes, stirring frequently, until very soft. Add the tomatoes, red kidney beans, chilli sauce and a little salt and simmer for 5 minutes until pulpy.

three Drain the squash from the stock, reserving the stock, and return to the pan. Scatter over the spinach leaves, cover and cook for about 1 minute until the spinach has wilted in the steam.

four Pile the vegetables on to steamed rice on serving plates. Stir 8 tablespoons of the reserved stock into the sauce with the coriander. Spoon over the vegetables and serve with soured cream and an avocado and lime salad if liked.

This is a great dish to make during the autumn, when various
baby squash and pumpkin are at their most plentiful.

A frittata is an Italian-style omelette and, like an omelette, can be flavoured in many interesting ways. For best results, use a good-quality, heavy-based, frying pan and really fresh, flavoursome eggs.

watercress and mushroom frittata

preparation time **5 mins**
cooking time **15 mins**
total time **20 mins** serves **3–4**

6 eggs
5 tablespoons grated Parmesan cheese
1 bunch of watercress, tough stalks removed
40 g/1½ oz butter
250 g/8 oz mushrooms, thinly sliced
salt and pepper

one Beat the eggs in a bowl with a fork to break them up. Stir in the Parmesan, watercress and plenty of salt and pepper.
two Melt the butter in a heavy-based frying pan. Add the mushrooms and fry quickly for 3 minutes. Pour in the egg mixture and gently stir the ingredients together.
three Reduce the heat to its lowest setting and fry gently until the mixture is lightly set and the underside is golden when the edge of the frittata is lifted with a palette knife. If the base of the frittata starts to catch before the top is set, place it under a moderate grill to finish cooking.

basil and tomato stew

preparation time **10 mins**
cooking time **15 mins**
total time **25 mins** serves **4**

1 kg/2 lb ripe tomatoes, skinned
6 tablespoons olive oil
2 onions, chopped
4 celery sticks, sliced
4 plump garlic cloves, thinly sliced
175 g/6 oz mushrooms, sliced
3 tablespoons sun-dried tomato paste
600 ml/1 pint Vegetable Stock (see page 9)
1 tablespoon muscovado sugar
3 tablespoons capers
large handful of basil leaves,
    about 15 g/½ oz
large handful of chervil or flat leaf parsley,
    about 15 g/½ oz
salt and pepper
warm bread, to serve

one Quarter and deseed the tomatoes, scooping out the pulp into a sieve over a bowl to catch the juices.
two Heat 4 tablespoons of the oil in a large saucepan and fry the onions and celery for 5 minutes. Add the garlic and mushrooms and fry for a further 3 minutes.
three Add the tomatoes and their juices, sun-dried tomato paste, stock, sugar and capers and bring to the boil. Reduce the heat and simmer gently, with the pan uncovered, for 5 minutes.
four Tear the herbs into pieces, add to the pan with a little salt and pepper and cook for 1 minute. Ladle into bowls, drizzle with the remaining oil and serve with warm bread.

baked vine tomatoes with garlic and herbs

preparation time **5 mins**
cooking time **20 mins**
total time **25 mins** serves **4**

500 g/1 lb vine-ripened tomatoes
2 plump garlic cloves, thinly sliced
1 tablespoon roughly chopped thyme
   or rosemary
2 red chillies, halved lengthways
5 tablespoons extra virgin olive oil
4 tablespoons balsamic vinegar
salt and pepper

one Cut the tomatoes from the vine in clumps of 2 or 3. Make a deep slit in each tomato and insert a couple of garlic slices, a good pinch of herbs and season to taste with salt and pepper. Pack into a shallow ovenproof dish.

two Tuck the chilli halves around the tomatoes. Pour over the oil and vinegar, and check the seasoning: you may need a little more salt and pepper. Bake in a preheated oven, 220°C (425°F), Gas Mark 7, for 20 minutes until the tomatoes are softened but not falling apart.

spaghetti squash with cabbage and nuts

Preparation time **10 mins**
Cooking time **20 mins**
Total time **30 mins** Serves **3–4**

1 spaghetti squash, weighing about
   1.5 kg/3 lb
40g/1½ oz butter
1 onion, thinly sliced
2 garlic cloves, crushed
150 g/5 oz green cabbage, finely shredded
75 g/3 oz natural peanuts or cashews
100 g/3½ oz crème fraîche
plenty of freshly grated nutmeg
salt and pepper

one Place the squash in a large pan in which it just fits. Cover with boiling water and boil for 20 minutes.

two Meanwhile, melt the butter in a frying pan and gently fry the onion and garlic for 5 minutes. Stir in the cabbage and fry for 3 minutes until tender. Add the nuts, crème fraîche, and nutmeg, season to taste with salt and pepper and cook until the crème fraîche melts to make a sauce.

three Drain and halve the spaghetti squash, and discard the seeds from the centre. Using 2 forks, shred the flesh into a bowl, breaking it up into fine threads. Add to the frying pan and toss the ingredients together over the heat for 1 minute. Serve immediately.

aubergine pâté

preparation time **10 mins**
cooking time **15 mins**
total time **25 mins** serves **6**

25 g/1 oz dried porcini mushrooms
500 g/1 lb aubergines
6 tablespoons olive oil
1 small red onion, chopped
2 teaspoons cumin seeds
175 g/6 oz cup or chestnut mushrooms
2 garlic cloves, crushed
3 pickled walnuts, halved
small handful of coriander
salt and pepper
toasted walnut or grainy bread, to serve

one Place the dried mushrooms in a bowl and cover with plenty of boiling water. Leave to soak for 10 minutes.

two Meanwhile, cut the aubergines into 1 cm/½ inch dice. Heat the oil in a large frying pan. Add the aubergines and onion and fry gently for 8 minutes until the vegetables are softened and browned.

three Drain the dried mushrooms and add to the pan with the cumin seeds, fresh mushrooms and garlic. Fry for a further 5–7 minutes until the aubergines are very soft.

four Transfer to a food processor or blender with the pickled walnuts and coriander, season to taste with salt and pepper and process until broken up but not completely smooth. Transfer to a serving dish and serve warm or cold with toast.

Just a few dried mushrooms really boost the flavour of this quick and easy pâté. It makes plenty and leftovers keep well in the refrigerator for several days, ready for either zipping up vegetable stews or spreading on to toast and grilling with Gruyère cheese.

vegetable crisps

preparation time **10 mins**
cooking time **5 mins**
total time **15 mins** serves **4–6**

250 g/8 oz each potato, parsnip and
   raw beetroot
oil, for deep-frying
coarse sea salt and pepper

one Cut the vegetables into very thin slices
using the slicer attachment of a food
processor or a mandoline. They can also
be sliced by hand, although it can be difficult
to get them sufficiently fine. Pat the
vegetables dry on kitchen paper.
two Pour the oil into a deep-fat fryer or
heavy-based saucepan until about a third
full. Heat the oil until a piece of vegetable
sizzles on the surface. Add a batch of
vegetable slices to the oil and fry until crisp
and golden. Drain on kitchen paper while
frying the remainder. Serve generously
seasoned with salt and pepper.

buttered cauliflower crumble

preparation time **8 mins**
cooking time **12 mins**
total time **20 mins** serves **4**

1 large cauliflower
25 g/1 oz butter
50 g/2 oz breadcrumbs
2 tablespoons olive oil
3 tablespoons capers
3 cocktail gherkins, finely chopped
3 tablespoons chopped dill or tarragon
100 g/3½ oz crème fraîche
4 tablespoons grated Parmesan cheese
salt and pepper

one Cut the cauliflower into large florets and
blanch in boiling water for 2 minutes. Drain
the florets thoroughly.
two Melt half of the butter in a large frying
pan. Add the breadcrumbs and fry for
2 minutes until golden. Drain and set aside.
three Melt the remaining butter in the pan
with the oil. Add the cauliflower florets and
fry gently for about 5 minutes until golden.
Add the capers, gherkins, dill or tarragon and
crème fraîche, season to taste with salt and
pepper and stir the mixture over a moderate
heat for 1 minute.
four Turn into a shallow flameproof dish
and sprinkle with the fried breadcrumbs
and Parmesan. Cook under a preheated
moderate grill for about 2 minutes until
the crumbs are dark golden brown.

pan-fried roots with cardamom and honey

preparation time **10 mins**
cooking time **15 mins**
total time **25 mins** serves **4**

275 g/9 oz small turnips, cut into wedges
1 small sweet potato, scrubbed and cut
    into chunks
275 g/9 oz medium parsnips, cut into wedges
8 shallots, peeled but left whole
1 tablespoon cardamom pods
2 tablespoons clear honey
2 teaspoons lemon juice
4 tablespoons olive oil
salt and pepper

one Cook the turnips, sweet potato, parsnips and shallots in lightly salted boiling water for 7–8 minutes until they are softened but not tender.

two Meanwhile, crush the cardamom pods using a pestle and mortar to release the seeds. Alternatively, crush the pods in a small bowl using the end of a rolling pin. Pick out and discard the pods, then pound the seeds to crush them slightly. Mix the crushed seeds with the honey, lemon juice and a little salt and pepper.

three Drain the vegetables. Heat the oil in a large frying pan. Add the vegetables and fry for about 6 minutes until golden, stirring frequently. Add the cardamom dressing and toss together for 1 minute. Serve hot.

Crushed cardamom seeds are delicious with root vegetables, bringing out their sweet, earthy flavours. Serve as an accompaniment to vegetable pancakes and spicy rice and bean dishes.

desserts and bakes

Simple cooking techniques such as pan-frying, baking and grilling capitalize on the many winning qualities of fresh, ripe fruits to create irresistible desserts with the minimum of time and fuss. Bakes, too, can be quick as well as rewarding to make, providing a ready supply of luxurious snacks and indulgent sweet treats.

cranberry, oatmeal and cinnamon scones

preparation time **10 mins**
cooking time **12 mins**
total time **22 mins** makes **10**

175 g/6 oz self-raising flour
1 teaspoon baking powder
1 teaspoon ground cinnamon
75 g/3 oz unsalted butter
75 g/3 oz caster sugar
50 g/2 oz oatmeal, plus extra for sprinkling
75 g/3 oz dried cranberries
5–6 tablespoons milk
beaten egg or milk, to glaze

one Grease a baking sheet. Place the flour, baking powder and cinnamon in a food processor. Add the butter, cut into small pieces, and process until the mixture resembles breadcrumbs. Add the sugar and oatmeal and blend briefly. Alternatively, use your fingertips to rub the butter into the flour, baking powder and cinnamon in a bowl, then add the sugar and oatmeal.

two Add the cranberries and milk and blend briefly until the mixture forms a soft dough, adding a little more milk if necessary.

three Turn out on to a floured surface and roll out to 1.5 cm/¾ inch thick. Cut out rounds using a 5 cm/2 inch cutter. Transfer to the prepared baking sheet and re-roll the trimmings to make more scones.

four Brush with beaten egg or milk and sprinkle with oatmeal. Bake in a preheated oven, 220°C (425°F), Gas Mark 7, for 10–12 minutes until risen and golden. Transfer to a wire rack to cool. Serve split and buttered.

Like all scones, these sweet fruit-specked ones are
best served freshly baked, or frozen ahead and
then thawed and warmed through to serve.

This unbelievably easy dessert is perfect for any occasion, whether you are entertaining friends or are in desperate need of something sweet and delicious.

plum and amaretto tartlets

preparation time **10 mins**
cooking time **15 mins**
total time **25 mins** serves **6**

375 g/12 oz puff pastry
a little beaten egg, to glaze
175 g/6 oz white or golden almond paste
icing sugar, for dusting
500 g/1 lb red or yellow plums, halved
    and stoned
4 tablespoons Amaretto liqueur or brandy
lightly whipped cream, to serve

one Lightly grease a baking sheet and sprinkle with water. Roll out the pastry on a lightly floured surface and cut out six 10 cm/4 inch rounds using a cutter or small saucer as a guide. Using the tip of a sharp knife, make a shallow cut 1 cm/½ inch from the edge of each round to form a rim. Brush the tops with beaten egg and transfer to the baking sheet.

two Roll out the almond paste on a surface dusted with icing sugar and cut out six 7 cm/3 inch rounds. Place a round in the centre of each tartlet. Arrange the plum halves over the almond paste, cut sides up, and drizzle with as much liqueur or brandy as the cavities will hold. Bake in a preheated oven, 220°C (425°F), Gas Mark 7, for about 15 minutes until the pastry is well risen.

three Spoon over any remaining liqueur and dust with icing sugar. Serve the tartlets with whipped cream.

chunky oat cookies

preparation time **10 mins**
cooking time **15 mins**
total time **25 mins** makes **15**

125 g/4 oz unsalted butter, softened
125 g/4 oz golden caster sugar
1 egg
2 teaspoons vanilla extract
125 g/4 oz porridge oats
4 tablespoons sunflower seeds
150 g/5 oz plain flour
½ teaspoon baking powder
175 g/6 oz white chocolate, chopped into
    small pieces
icing sugar, for dusting

one Lightly grease a large baking sheet.
Beat together the butter and sugar in a bowl
until creamy. Add the egg, vanilla, oats,
sunflower seeds, flour and baking powder
and mix together to make a thick paste. Stir
in the chocolate pieces.
two Place dessertspoonfuls of the mixture
on the prepared baking sheet and flatten
slightly with the back of a fork.
three Bake in a preheated oven, 180°C
(350°F), Gas Mark 4, for about 15 minutes
until risen and golden. Leave for 5 minutes,
then transfer to a wire rack to cool. Serve
dusted with icing sugar.

Use good-quality white chocolate
without the oversweet, cloying taste
of cheaper chocolate, or use milk or
plain chocolate if preferred.

quick tiramisu

preparation time **15 mins**, plus chilling
total time **15 mins** serves **4–6**

5 tablespoons strong espresso coffee
75 g/3 oz dark muscovado sugar
4 tablespoons coffee liqueur or
    3 tablespoons brandy
75 g/3 oz sponge finger biscuits,
    broken into large pieces
400 g/13 oz good-quality ready-made custard
250 g/8 oz mascarpone cheese
1 teaspoon vanilla extract
50 g/2 oz plain chocolate, finely chopped
cocoa powder, for dusting

one Mix the coffee with 2 tablespoons
of the sugar and the liqueur or brandy in
a medium bowl. Toss the sponge fingers
in the mixture and turn into a serving dish,
spooning over any excess liquid.
two Beat together the custard, mascarpone
and vanilla and spoon a third over the
biscuits. Sprinkle with the remaining sugar,
then half the remaining custard. Scatter with
the chopped chocolate, then spread with the
remaining custard.
three Chill for about 1 hour until set. Serve
dusted with cocoa powder.

pan-fried apricots with gingered mascarpone

preparation time **5 mins**
cooking time **3 mins**
total time **8 mins** serves **4**

2 pieces of bottled stem ginger
2 tablespoons syrup from the ginger jar
250 g/8 oz mascarpone cheese
2 teaspoons lemon juice
50 g/2 oz unsalted butter
25 g/1 oz light muscovado sugar
400 g/13 oz fresh apricots, halved
3 tablespoons Amaretto liqueur or brandy

one Finely chop the stem ginger and mix with the ginger syrup, mascarpone and lemon juice.
two Melt the butter in a frying pan and add the sugar. Cook for about 1 minute until the sugar has dissolved. Add the apricots and fry quickly until lightly coloured but still firm. Stir in the liqueur or brandy.
three Spoon the mascarpone on to serving plates, top with the fruit and juices and serve the dessert warm.

grilled peaches with brown sugar brûlée

preparation time **5 mins**
cooking time **5 mins**
total time **10 mins** serves **4**

4 large juicy peaches
150 ml/¼ pint double cream
2 teaspoons lemon juice
3 tablespoons unrefined icing sugar
1 tablespoon flaked almonds

one Halve the peaches, remove the stones and place, skin sides down, in a shallow flameproof dish.
two Mix the cream with the lemon juice and 1 tablespoon of the icing sugar. Pour over the peaches. Sprinkle with the remaining icing sugar, then the almonds.
three Cook under a preheated moderate grill for about 5 minutes until the sugar is bubbling and lightly caramelized. Serve warm.

A simple dessert that makes the most of fresh apricots during their all-too-short season. When they are not available, it is equally good made with red or yellow plums. Amaretti or ratafia biscuits make a no-fuss accompaniment.

toffee apple bake

preparation time **10 mins**
cooking time **20 mins**
total time **30 mins** serves **4**

3 dessert apples, cored and thickly sliced
100 g/3½ oz self-raising flour, plus
    1 tablespoon extra
125 g/4 oz light muscovado sugar
50 g/2 oz caster sugar
½ teaspoon ground mixed spice
1 egg
100 ml/3½ fl oz natural yogurt
50 g/2 oz unsalted butter, melted

one Toss the apples in a shallow ovenproof
dish with 1 tablespoonful of the flour and
the muscovado sugar.
two Mix the remaining flour with the caster
sugar and spice in a bowl. Add the egg,
yogurt and butter and stir lightly until only
just combined.
three Spoon the mixture over the prepared
apples and bake in a preheated oven,
220°C (425°F), Gas Mark 7, for about
15–20 minutes until just firm and golden.
Serve warm.

A great standby that few can
resist! During cooking, the
muscovado sugar melts to
form a deliciously smooth,
toffee-like sauce for the apples.
It is perfect served with vanilla
ice cream.

blueberry and vanilla muffins

preparation time **5 mins**
cooking time **15 mins**
total time **20 mins** makes **10**

150 g/5 oz ground almonds
150 g/5 oz golden caster sugar
50 g/2 oz self-raising flour
175 g/6 oz unsalted butter, melted
4 egg whites
1 teaspoon vanilla extract
150 g/5 oz blueberries

one Line 10 sections of a muffin tray with
paper cases, or grease the sections. Mix
together the ground almonds, sugar, flour
and butter. Add the egg whites and vanilla
extract and mix to a smooth paste.
two Spoon into the cases and scatter with
the blueberries.
three Bake in a preheated oven, 220°C (425°F),
Gas Mark 7, for 15 minutes until just firm in
the centre. Leave for 5 minutes, then transfer
the muffins to a wire rack to cool.

You need luscious, full-flavoured dessert pears, which
will soften quickly in the syrup, to make this pudding.

syrupy pears with chocolate crumble

preparation time **5 mins**
cooking time **8 mins**
total time **13 mins** serves **4**

50 g/2 oz light muscovado sugar
25 g/1 oz raisins
½ teaspoon ground cinnamon
4 ripe dessert pears, peeled, halved
    and cored
40 g/1½ oz unsalted butter
50 g/2 oz porridge oats
25 g/1 oz hazelnuts, roughly chopped
50 g/2 oz plain or milk chocolate, chopped
lightly whipped cream or Greek yogurt,
    to serve (optional)

one Place half of the sugar in a frying pan or wide sauté pan with 150 ml/¼ pint water and the raisins and cinnamon. Bring just to the boil, add the pears and simmer gently, uncovered, for about 5 minutes until the pears are slightly softened.
two Melt the butter in a separate frying pan or saucepan. Add the porridge oats and fry gently for 2 minutes. Stir in the remaining sugar and cook over a gentle heat until golden.
three Spoon the pears on to serving plates. Stir the hazelnuts and chocolate into the oats mixture. Once the chocolate starts to melt, spoon over the pears. Serve topped with whipped cream or Greek yogurt if liked.

chocolate cherry slices

preparation time **10 mins**
total time **10 mins** serves **4**

425 g/14 oz can black cherries in syrup
3 tablespoons Kirsch
1 tablespoon lemon juice
100 g/3½ oz ricotta cheese
2 tablespoons icing sugar
25 g/1 oz plain chocolate, chopped
1 piece of bottled stem ginger, finely chopped
4 thick slices of moist chocolate cake

one Thoroughly drain the cherries, reserving the syrup. Blend 4 tablespoons of the syrup with the Kirsch and lemon juice.
two Mix together the ricotta and icing sugar in a bowl. Gently fold in the cherries, chocolate and ginger.
three Place the chocolate cake on serving plates and spoon over the Kirsch syrup. Pile the cherry mixture on top.

Bought chocolate cake can be dramatically transformed when bathed in liqueured syrup and topped with cherries, ricotta and chocolate chunks.

Index

Acknowledgements

Executive Editor: Sarah Ford
Project Editor: Alice Tyler
Executive Art Editor: Geoff Fennell
Designer: Sue Michniewicz

Photographer: William Reavell
Stylist: Clare Hunt
Home Economist: Joanna Farrow
Production Controller: Ian Paton